Student Success Principles

Increase Confidence, Lower Student Debt, and Find a Career You Love

Contents

FREE Bonuses

Along with this book I wanted to give you some bonuses to help you as you complete the book. The bonuses I have created are:

1. A life assessment wheel

2. A time management chart

3. A 30-day goal checklist

4. Access to my live video discussions starting November 2019!

   - If you get your bonuses before November, I will invite you to join me live for deeper discussions on my book and the student success principles

5. My resume template

You will see references to these throughout the book. If you want to take a sneak peek now, you can go to StudentSuccessPrinciples.com and grab them today!

Introduction

"The only person you are destined to become

Is the person you decide to be"

- **Ralph Waldo Emerson**

High school is hard and college can be pretty difficult. Anybody that says any different is lying to you! Every year there are plenty of students struggling and they have to learn what it takes to graduate from high school or college. The big question is: Why does it have to be so hard? We have spent anywhere from thirteen to twenty or more years in school, but none of it really prepares us for stepping out into the real world. You know graduation is coming, but *how* do you navigate the life after that?

When I was in high school, I thought I had it all figured out. I thought I knew what college I was going to, what I'd be majoring in, who'd I'd be hanging out with. I knew I had to go to college, but not fully understanding *why*. All I knew was "to get a good job you have to go to college." I didn't quite know the how or the why. My friends also seemed to have similar things on their minds.

I worked very hard in my junior and senior years in school. I took the ACT and SAT multiple times. I spent a lot of time down at the school counselor's office trying to find as many scholarships as I could to help pay for college. I didn't really have a timeline of when I needed to have everything done, so I was trying to do everything at once. I at least knew I was going to go to *some* school and major in something like engineering.

In school I tried to be a part of as many clubs as I could. I got good grades. I looked at schools while also balancing a social life and a part-time job after school. It was all a big rush with one big, but vague goal—get into college.

As I started the second half of my senior year, I had my choice narrowed down to three schools: Ohio State University, Youngstown State University—a local commuter college—and The University of Akron. I was balancing out costs, the "coolness" factor, and everyone I knew who would be going to those colleges. It was exciting imagining who I would be spending my time with and all of the fun I would be having once I got into college. Little did I know that all of my choices would be changing on a cold day in March.

I had just finished talking to my parents about the

different colleges that I was dreaming of going to. We were planning visits and figuring out the requirements for all of the schools. I then went over to my girlfriend's house to spend some time with her on my day off from work. As I walked into her bedroom, I could see that she was incredibly upset, crying, and from the look in her eyes I knew something was definitely wrong. That is when she mumbled the two words that would drastically change my future.

"I'm pregnant."

When I first heard it, I could not fully believe it. I thought, *This can't happen to us, we have plans for the future. We're good people. I'm only eighteen! How am I going to handle this?*

My mind raced through a lot of different scenarios on how two people, who were practically kids ourselves, were going to bring a new human into this world while trying to achieve a successful future.

As weeks went by, thoughts of which school I was going to turned into thoughts about where the baby was going to stay, what things we would need to buy, and how in the hell I was going to tell my parents.

You see, my parents thought very highly of me. They are great parents who truly love me, and they could see all of my potential. They knew I was bound for greatness in my future.

They wanted me to go to the best college and get the best grades, which would lead to a great job. How do I tell my parents that our future was not going to be the same?

After a month or so of avoiding real talks with my parents and carrying a large amount of stress on my shoulders, I finally told them everything. I was so nervous I had to write a letter and leave it for them to find when they came home from work. That was easily one of the longest days of my life. Waiting all day for them to call. Wondering how they would react. Wondering what they would say. Knowing that they would be upset killed me inside.

After they called and I got off work, the drive home to have the dreaded talk seemed to take forever. As we sat there and cried, we talked about the future and what could come of it. For a few weeks, it was very difficult to talk about because a lot of the choices I had at the top of my list were changing. I wasn't able to go to school three hours away and leave my child behind. The only suitable decision I could make was for me to stay at home and go to Youngstown State University, our local commuter school.

Thinking about the future was very stressful, but I knew in my heart that I had to move forward and I wasn't going to let having a baby at eighteen ruin my future. I knew that if I put enough time and energy into everything, I could still succeed. It might not be the exact path that I was planning, but the endpoint was going to be the same.

My girlfriend and I broke up shortly after our son was born. I knew we weren't right for each other and didn't want to stay together just because of him. It added more stress to our lives, but we both pushed forward with our college careers. I wanted to make sure I was the best dad, student, and worker I could be.

Through many fights, late nights, and long days, I pushed through graduation with two degrees. Halfway through my college career I realized I was not as passionate about engineering as I thought I was. I finished my associate's in engineering and switched my major to computer science. After five years of school, while taking one semester off for an internship, I was able to graduate with an associate's degree in engineering and a bachelor's degree in information technology. All of this while still having my son on weekends and balancing work in between.

Not only did I graduate with two degrees, but I was actually able to secure a job three months before graduation, which was sixty miles away from my house and college. I drove to downtown Cleveland every day and two days a week I had to drive back to school in the afternoon to finish my afternoon classes. It wasn't ideal, but knowing I had employment waiting for me right after graduation was great.

Because of my work and dedication to my job, the

company started sending me to England to work on a big project. I would travel there one or two weeks at a time, then travel back to spend time with my son and girlfriend on the weekends. It was a busy time in my life, but I was grateful to have successfully made it through graduation and land a great job thanks to my degree.

I tell you all of this because I want you to know that it is all possible. Life is always going to throw you curves, but it is possible. It will take a lot of hard work, but if you have the dedication you can do anything you want to. I know that is a cliché that a lot of people like to throw around, but they are usually people who don't believe it. I'm living proof, though, that you can and *will* push through challenges that come your way.

I have been working as a software engineer for five years now. I increased my income by over fifty percent in the first three years of working and I continue to grow within my company. I was also able to move to Charleston, South Carolina, after my son moved down with his mom a few years ago.

***

I am living the life that I used to dream about. As I have grown, so have my dreams. I plan to continue to grow and accomplish bigger and better things. I am hoping that you can learn from my successes. As I continue my career as a software engineer, my passions and purpose have changed. I want to help students succeed in their future. By helping students as they move forward into becoming an adult, I don't want them to stumble. I want them to excel. Imagine what our world would be like if you stumbled less and excelled more!

I wrote this book because I want to lower the learning curve of high school and college students for success after graduation. There are way too many students graduating high school with confusion and fear on what to do afterwards as they prepare for the workforce or college. There are too many college graduates that have degrees that cost tens of thousands of dollars, who end up with jobs that barely pay the rent.

We spend our entire school career learning from textbooks in order to pass tests. With some hard work, we pass those tests with the hopes that will lead to a great job. What we don't learn, however, are the skills it takes to secure those great jobs. How to handle our finances. How to shop for houses. How to work through new challenges. How to deal with coworkers.

It shouldn't take years after graduation to figure it out. We've already spent over thirteen years leading up to graduation and becoming an adult. Why should we spend another two or five years learning how to *be* an adult? Many would argue they are still learning how to "adult" ten years later!

This book is written for high school and college students, as well as parents. I want to assist with eliminating the guesswork and change your mindset from one of confusion about life after graduation to that of confidence about how successful you'll be.

In this book I will cover topics about getting into college, adulting, finances, as well as personal development. Personal development is without a doubt the number one thing that brought me to where I am today. I was stuck in the mindset of "take the next class, hit the next step, graduate, get the job." What I didn't realize was that in order to succeed, I really needed to become a better version of myself.

This book will change the way you think of yourself as a person—and potentially, the way you look at the world. This isn't about just graduating with a job. This is about finding out WHO you are meant to be and figuring out how to get there. Anybody can just graduate, but who you become during that time is what sets you up for your future.

So join me on your journey to success after graduation! Take this first step to a better future and a better *you*. If you are a parent reading this book, I encourage you to have your teenager read this too. I also recommend that you read this book first so you can fully explain the emotions and lessons they may experience as a result of the information I present.

Personal Development

Getting to Know Yourself

"If you don't like the road you're walking,

start paving another one"

-Dolly Parton

Before we can think about success after graduation, we need to figure out exactly what you plan on doing after school. If you think you already know what that is, that's fine, but I urge you to read this chapter. It may make you rethink what you want to do. I want you to think deeply about what you will be doing after graduation. I want you to be passionate about it and enjoy it!

Self-Awareness

If you google *self-awareness* you will see a definition of "conscious knowledge of one's own character, feelings, motives, and desires." A lot of us go through life day by day, not really paying attention to who we are as a person.

We may think highly or not so highly of ourselves, but we don't really know what makes us, *us*.

Having self-awareness is a great skill to have. Have you ever met someone that doesn't know some of their own bad traits? You may think to yourself, *How could they ever act like that? Do they not realize how they come across?* Most of the time, they don't. I don't want you to be like that, I want you to self-evaluate and find your strengths and weaknesses.

This evaluation isn't something you can just complete in a few minutes. This may take some time. You may even have to ask others for help. To start, I want you to get a piece of paper and write down the following questions:

First, we will start off with **strengths**:

~ What are some things I am good at?

~ What are some things that come naturally?

~ What are things that people come to me for help with?

~ What are things that I do without much effort?

Some answers might be friendships, sports, school, listening, and technology. Spend some time looking at this. If you can, ask some friends or family members what some of the things you do are and what they look up to you for. We all have strengths, but sometimes we do not really see what those are. We use them every day, but don't realize others look at those as strengths.

Weaknesses

Weaknesses might be a little easier. These might point themselves out as you attempt to come up with skills to accomplish different tasks. Write these questions down:

~ What are some things I struggle with?
~ What are some things I ask for help with from my friends?
~ What are some things I avoid doing because they are difficult?
~ What are some things that make me uncomfortable when asked to do them?

This is another area that asking friends and family to help with would be a good idea. You might have even found it easy to write these weaknesses down. As humans, we tend to focus on what we do *not* do well compared to what we *do*, do well. Some of these answers might be in the list I mentioned earlier. In every area of life, some people have strengths in one area, while that area might be a weakness to others.

This might be obvious in groups of friends. There are obvious similarities within your group of friends, but I'm sure some friends are better at some things than others. Good groups of friends help each other, though. I am one of the go-to friends when it comes to computers and organizing group activities.

I go to another friend for graphic design help. I go to another friend for investment help. I am perfectly happy to go to them because I would much rather ask someone who has strengths in an area instead of me struggling to *maybe* do a good job at something.

Weaknesses are not necessarily a bad thing, but it is good to know what they are so you can adjust situations around them. You do not want to go into a career that requires skills in an area you may have some weaknesses. We can always grow our weaknesses, but I prefer to really excel using my strengths.

Passions

Your passions will most likely come from your strengths. It is not very often you thoroughly enjoy doing something you are not great at. Write these questions down:

~ What makes me happy?

~ What are my favorite things to do in my down time?

~ If I could do one thing over and over forever, what would it be?

~ What is something I look forward to when people ask me to do it?

These are some of my favorite questions. I enjoy reflecting on my passions because they tend to be related to helping people, and I am good at them. That is why my friends might come to me more often than others. That is why I am writing this book and working with students. I want students to succeed after graduation, not just stumble through hoping for an *okay* job when they move on from high school.

I discovered more about my passion and personal development after getting through school and graduating. I am realizing that this information could have helped me more through school. I do not regret going through college and getting my two degrees. I am much more knowledgeable because of it. I also have a great-paying job from it, which is helping me take care of finances and live the lifestyle that I have always wanted. I picked a career path in school based on what I enjoyed. My passions have shifted. Or maybe they became more obvious, but I was able to get a job doing something I enjoy, and getting paid on top of that is a bonus!

So why am I focusing so much on self-awareness and your passions? I want you to find your passions, because passions lead to motivation. When you have motivation to pursue something, it makes it a lot easier to achieve your goals.

Think about school. I'm sure you don't enjoy writing long papers or completing large projects. If the due date is given to you two weeks out, when do you finish the paper? The night before, right? The motivation of getting a good grade isn't quite strong enough to get you to start it earlier and spend more time on it.

I was a huge procrastinator in school. My papers were usually written a day or two before they were due, in between anything else I could do that was more interesting to me. Did my grades suffer sometimes? Of course they did, but I kept a strong eye on my grades and would balance my time accordingly. Now I have a job doing what I enjoy. I almost never procrastinate on my work because I enjoy programming and learning new things along the way.

This is why I want you to find your passions. These passions will one, help you go through school easier since you will be learning new information about something you enjoy. Two, when you graduate and get a job in the field, you will be working at least forty hours a week doing something you love. You may have a job right now that you don't exactly love. Do you ever realize how it is sometimes difficult to get out of bed to go to work? Maybe you have parents that don't like their job and you hear how disappointed they get when it comes time to get ready for work. Or maybe you hear them on Sundays dreading the work week that starts again on Monday.

When you pick a career path, you could potentially be picking something you will be doing for a large part of your life. I'm not saying you can't change your path throughout your life, but it takes time and a lot of hard work to switch to something completely different. What if you started it right from the beginning? What if, on most days, you enjoyed going to work?

Balance

One thing I must caution you on is seeing how practical your passion is. I highly encourage people to go into a field doing something they love, but you also need to balance the job market around that passion. If you absolutely love swimming and could do it every day for the rest of your life, what type of job can you do with that? I know there is a really great job as a mermaid in Florida, and maybe a few others that would require swimming, but finding those could be very difficult.

I also do not want you going into a field *just* because it pays well or has a large job market. Computer programming is hiring all over the place. Hospitals are looking for doctors everywhere. Do not go into those fields if you do not like computers or freak out at the sight of blood.

One common idea I hear from students is joining the National Guard because they will pay for your college. I highly respect the National Guard, and would urge you to investigate it, but *only* if you have a passion for joining it and want to serve your country. Joining just because they pay for your college could be a big mistake. You are signing up for four years of something that you do not have a real passion for. You could be miserable for those four years just so you can get money for college, which you will have to spend another four years at anyway. There are easier ways to make money, which I will cover in a later chapter.

Now, let's say you do some research on jobs related to your passion and there isn't really a big job market for it. What do you do then? You should try to look at a career path that you will still enjoy and that has a good job market. There is so much information out there that describes what typical jobs are like in each industry/field. It might not be a direct reflection of your passions, but you can still use some of your top skills in that job.

When it comes time to apply to the job, you'll want to get one at a place that will still allow you to enjoy your passion outside of work. That is what I'm doing now. I am working as a computer programmer at a company that gives me flexible hours. After I get out of work I work on content and meeting new people to further expand by business.

Glassdoor is a great resource to research culture at a company. Look to see what employees are saying about work/life balance. Look for high ratings for the types of positions you are looking for at the company. You can find companies that have good work/life balance and a fun culture.

It is a lot easier working at a place when you enjoy being there.

Gaining Experience

At this point, we have found out what your strengths are and what you are passionate about. Now it is time to test these out and experience your passions! If you are in college, the best way to get experience is through an internship. I will go deeper into internships later in this book, but they are without a doubt the best way to experience your career path. The other experience I am talking about is shadowing or learning from someone who is already in that field.

It is one thing to think something is good for you and read about it in a book. It is another thing to get information directly from people who are working in your desired field. They can give you information on what daily responsibilities and duties entail as well as insight on how much of what they learn in school is *actually* used in their job. If you can, see if you can go into their place of work with them one day to see what a day in the life looks like.

I originally thought I was going to be a mechanical engineer. I was able to take some engineering prep classes to get a feel for engineering work, and I really enjoyed those classes. Unfortunately, as I got into college, things started to shift. I realized that I would be spending more time on calculation than designing. Admittingly, some of my professors weren't providing me with the greatest view into what the engineering world is *really* like. Eventually, after I earned my associate's, I changed my major from engineering to information technology.

I know today that was the best decision I could have made. Luckily, I was still able to graduate with two degrees after a total of five years in school, which is not really any more time than an average four-year degree (most four-year degrees take more than four years to attain, unfortunately).

My point is, the experiences I had in college made me realize that engineering was not quite for me. My internship for information technology also made me realize that I actually wanted to go into programming. I was originally going to look at computer networking, but when I went to my internship and spent three months writing software for that company, I found out how much I actually enjoyed programming. I would not have realized this without my internship.

Visualize

I now want you to visualize your future using your passions and strengths. Imagine what type of job you'll have. What you'll be doing. What your paycheck may look like. What type of lifestyle you will have. What your day-to-day life will entail. Hopefully thinking of these things brings you happiness. If it doesn't, you may want to re-evaluate what you are planning to go into.

Now if, after reading this chapter, you do not fully know what you want to do with your future, that is perfectly okay! You have time to figure this out, even if you have already started college. The good thing is, in college, you can get all of the general education classes out of the way before you start on core classes for a major.

If you are in high school, you may find out that college is not the path you want to take, which is more than acceptable. I know plenty of people that have great jobs fulfilling their passion and they either didn't go to college at all, or they dropped out within the first year.

Your life is going to be filled with challenges and changes. It is how you react to those challenges that affects your future. If you are not looking to go on to college, you should still have a plan. What are you going to do to become successful in the workforce? You'll need to rise up to become one of the top employees on your team, or in your company. If you have a plan, you can truly be successful. Just find out where you want to end up and do whatever it takes to get there!

You have a long life in front of you, with plenty of room

for different paths. You might not always choose the right one, but make sure that you learn from it. As long as you are doing something you enjoy that supports you and your family, you will be successful with your life.

***

Finding out who you are can really help guide you to who you can become. Many people don't really pay attention to themselves and just move through each day not realizing where they are going or where they have been. After this chapter, hopefully you have started taking a look at yourself. Ideally, you are happy with who you currently are. If you aren't entirely happy with who you see in the mirror, you can begin making changes today to start moving towards who you want to become.

Summary

✓ Do a self-audit on your strengths.

✓ Discover your passions.

✓ Identify growth opportunities

Goal Setting

"If you fail to plan, you are planning to fail"

-Benjamin Franklin

Every year hundreds of thousands of people set New Year resolutions. Every year over eighty[1] percent of those people fail at accomplishing their goals. It becomes a repetitive cycle that never seems to get better. I really believe that needs to change.

Goals are something we always talk about. Whether it be goals at school, personal goals, or goals at work. It has become a "thing" that people talk about, but don't really put much value behind. People think, *No one else accomplishes their goals, so I am no worse than they are.* Just because others make it seem normal does not mean that it is the right way to think about it.

If someone asks you to lay out your goals for the next month or year, I am sure the last thing that comes to mind is "This is going to be fun!" Why is that? We have been pressured by social media that we *have* to come up with some goal and that goal has to make us so much better than what we are. We copy others' goals of exercising more, eating healthier, dropping bad habits, or whatever else you can think of. The problem is—those are not really the goals we *want*. We then wonder why a month later we are looking at ourselves in the mirror, thinking we have failed.

It doesn't have to be that way!

In this chapter I want you to re-think the way you look at goals. I want you to be excited about growing yourself. I want you to look at a goal and feel it in your *soul,* that this goal is going to make a big difference in your life. You will be so excited that your friends are going to look at you funny. They will think you are some crazy hippie that believes in magic.

Looking back

Before we start thinking about your future goals, I want you to look back on your past. I want you to think about who you are today and what has made you who you are.

Everything you have done up until this point has made you the person that you are; everything you do from today and moving forward will guide you to who you become in the future.

Our life is filled with ups and downs. Unfortunately, we only seem to focus on the negatives. When I speak to students, I ask them to share some of their wins over the past year. For some reason, they always have a hard time remembering the wins. They can easily list all of the small failures that seem to make the year a "bad year." They look forward to leaving the year behind and starting a new one. However, one year later, nothing has changed.

If you want to know what will work in the future, you need to know what is working *now* and grow on that. Think about times when you were at your best. Maybe you aced an exam or scored a winning goal for your team. Maybe a friend came to you for help because they trusted you and you were able to help them. Whatever it is, something led to that moment. Use that as momentum going forward.

Use Passion

As I mentioned earlier, creating goals just because it seems like the right thing to do usually does not end up how you would expect it to.

What is it about New Year resolutions that makes people think they can go from sitting on a couch binging Netflix to being able to run five days a week just because they put a new calendar on the wall? If you don't like running, making a goal and *forcing* yourself to run more is not going to make you suddenly fall in love with running. In fact, you will probably end up hating it and staying far away from it.

I am not saying running more is a bad goal. But doing it just because your friend said you should, for example, makes it a bad goal. If you truly want to see yourself change, get in shape, eat healthier, or do better in school. Do it because you know it will make you a better person and help you work towards becoming a better version of who you want to be. That is how you start a goal.

Assess Yourself

I want you to spend some time analyzing the different areas in your life and find out where you see room for improvement. Look at the chart below to view the different areas that create your life and use it to measure where you think you are in each of them. Some of these areas may have no value to you, and that is fine. Others are going to stick out and pique your interest.

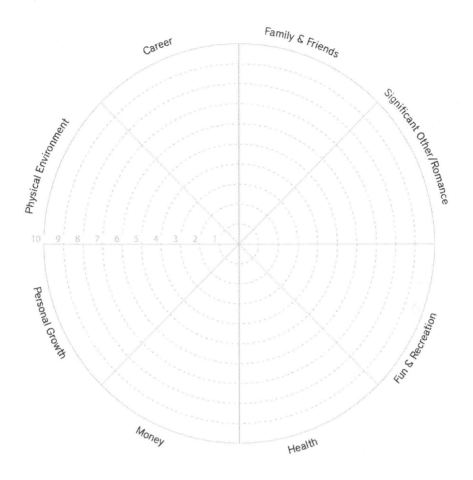

Career

Family & Friends

Significant Other/Romance

Physical Environment

10 9 8 7 6 5 4 3 2 1

Personal Growth

Fun & Recreation

Money

Health

You can download your own version at StudentSuccessPrinciples.com

These are the areas in your life we need to focus on because they'll assist with creating passion and fulfillment as you try to improve in them. Be honest with yourself. If your main food group is pizza, chicken, and burgers, don't say you are a level nine or ten in that area!

Don't be too hard on yourself if you realize you score low in some areas. This is what we are here to improve. If you don't have a metric to look at, you won't be able to know how much progress you have made. Seth Godin has a quote: "If you measure it, it will improve." I am sure you are better at some things now than you were five years ago. How much better are you? Could you measure it? How long did it take to improve? I bet if you were keeping track and measuring your progress, you would have improved quicker.

Creating the Goal

Now comes the fun part! Now that you are aware of some areas that need improvement, you can create goals that will help you get better in them. Like I said, if you don't really value a certain area, don't feel that you have to create a goal around it. If you don't want to increase your charitable giving (or don't have the money to do so), leave that area alone for now. We are creating goals that we *want* to do, not goals that someone else says we *need* to do.

Writing it Down

Here comes one of the biggest tips that a lot of people don't do. In fact, according to a Harvard Study[2], only three percent of Americans actually write down their goals.

Is it a coincidence that so many of us don't accomplish our goals and so few write them down? I think not!

Writing goals down makes them more real. More permanent. Keeping goals in your head is easy because they can change or easily disappear. Writing a goal down adds visualization. Once it is written down, you can put this goal somewhere in your house so you can look at it every day. Seeing a goal first thing in the morning as you wake up can help set an intention for the day.

In each area you want to improve in, create one or two high-level goals that will help you reach a level nine or ten in that area. As you start creating these goals, you may realize they are related to each other. This works out great because you can grow multiple areas of your life by doing the same thing.

In a perfect world, you will have *one* large goal that will help raise all (or at least a majority) of the areas in your life. One of my favorite books is *The ONE Thing*. It is an entire book dedicated to creating ONE goal that by achieving it, will make everything else easier.

Making a Plan

"A goal without a plan is just a wish."

– Antoine De Saint Exupery

Have you ever been on a road trip before? Do you just start driving with the hopes of finding your way to the end?

No. You use a GPS that lays out the entire path for you. Unfortunately, there is not a magical app that can tell you each and every step it will take to achieve your goal, but you can at least come up with a rough draft.

In order to create an action plan, you are going to need some form of a measurable metric to get there. If you want to lose weight, you need to set up how often you will be going to the gym and about how long it will take for you to get there.

Let's say you want to lose ten pounds over three months. That is just over three pounds per month. Break that down into a weekly goal and figure out what your diet should look like, as well as an exercise schedule.

If you want to get better grades, figure out what final grade you want and what it will take to raise it. Schedule out more studying or tutoring and keep track of where your grades are. As you progress through the grading period, you will see where you are and will have to adjust your plan along the way.

Go back and look at the goals you wrote out for yourself. After each section where you have a goal written down, I want you to write down a short and simple statement (one or two sentences) about *how* you are going to achieve those goals.

Here is an example I have for writing this book:

I am going to publish my first book this year by getting

the first rough draft done in thirty days. I will then follow up with editing and marketing over the next two months.

You may notice I put a timeline around my goal as well as a plan. If you don't have a deadline it will never get done. When you have a school paper due, when do you do it? The last day before it's due! If you give yourself small incremental due dates, you'll be able to knock out small steps one at a time, getting you closer to your goal. I don't care if there are ten steps or one thousand steps between you and your end goal. If you don't take one small step at a time, you will never reach the end.

Focus on Your Goals

At this point, you should have a full sheet (or sheets) of paper with two to five goals written down as well as a plan of attack. Put this somewhere you can look at on a daily, weekly, and monthly basis. Writing it down is a big part, but that doesn't magically make the goal come to life.

The more you look at your goals and truly focus on them, the quicker they will become a reality. Think about your life today and what you focus most of your attention on. It might be family, friends, school, or video games. Because you have a passion and spend time on that passion every day, it gets done and you improve in those areas. I want your end goal to be a part of *who you are*, not just some side thing you don't pay attention to.

Getting Things Done

I know that focusing on a goal that can help transform you might be new, but I promise it can and will help you grow in a positive way. I have accomplished quite a bit in my short life. Things I never thought I would be able to achieve. It took extreme focus but in my heart, I knew that by pushing forward one step at a time, I could achieve the things I set my mind to.

I created a 30-day goal setting checklist for you. Download it along with other bonuses at StudentSucessPrinciples.com

Summary

- ✓ Reflect and look back on what works
- ✓ Find your passion and who you are
- ✓ Assess areas in your life that need improvement
- ✓ Create goals around the areas you value and need improvement
- ✓ Write it down
    - ➢ Create a plan
    - ➢ Keep focus on your goals

Time Management

"Either run the day, or the day runs you"

- Jim Rohn

In school, we have a lot of time commitments we are constantly juggling. Classes, studying, work, social life, sleep. If you do not know how to manage these commitments, life can become stressful very quickly. Sometimes we don't balance well because we don't know how to. Other times we don't manage time well because we are really bad at it. Some of us don't look at time as something we manage, but as something that happens to us or something we have no control over.

Time is the one thing that everyone in the world has an equal amount of. We all have 24 hours in a day, or 168 hours in a week. Once the time passes, we can't get it back. We don't always realize how important or precious time is.

We typically just spend our time how we want. Of course, there are some responsibilities that require our time whether we like it or not, but how are you spending your time outside of those responsibilities?

Have you ever said to yourself that there is never enough time in a day? After saying that, did you ever look back and see exactly where you spent your time? I am sure there are some days you truly could not have squeezed much extra time out of your day. You woke up, went to school, work, studied, finished homework, and next thing you knew, you looked up and the day was over. How about the days leading up to that? Could you have maybe prepared a little more or spread out responsibilities throughout the week?

One of my favorite questions to ask someone after they say there is not enough time in a day is, "Have you ever sat down and binge-watched an entire season of a show on Netflix in one or two sittings?" The answer is almost always a hesitant "Yes." You see, in most cases we don't have a time problem, we have a time *management* problem. And if you do not pay attention and actually *evaluate* how you are spending your time, the problem will not get any better.

According to Tech Crunch[3], we spend nearly *six hours a day* watching TV and almost an hour a day on social networking sites.

Think about that for a minute. That is almost an entire workday's worth of time with our eyes tied to a screen that could be used on more important things. Now I am not saying having a lazy day here and there is a bad thing. I completely understand lazy days and hangovers happen (for those of you that are legally allowed to drink!), but what about other days when you should be doing something better?

So why is time management so important to grasp during school? Your time responsibilities only increase as you get older. When you get a job, eight straight hours are taken away—guaranteed! Add in your commute, getting ready for the day, responsibilities, etc. Your extra time to get things done quickly slips away.

Now, when it comes to school projects, when do you usually get them done? The night before they are due? That doesn't usually fly at work. When you have a project or responsibility at your job, usually multiple people are depending on that to be done on time, or even earlier in some cases. It can't just be done with minimal effort quickly right before it's needed. Not to mention, chances are you will be juggling multiple responsibilities or projects at the same time. If you don't know how to manage your time well, you are going to have a hard time successfully getting your work done.

How to Improve Your

Time Management Skills

I have laid out some of the problems you may have with time management. Most of these issues are very common with college students as well as anyone ten years into their career. Have you ever met someone that never seems to have enough time and is always rushing? They may be given too many responsibilities, but chances are they need to improve their time management skills. I want to help you look at some ways you can become a time management ninja! I want you to be the person, that when people need help with something, they come to you because they know you are capable of getting things done. This skill will pay off greatly in your career and really, in all parts of your life!

1. Do a Time Audit on Yourself

It is hard to know where you can improve unless you evaluate how you currently spend your time. Before we look at areas that need improvement, let's look at times where you rocked at managing your time.

Think back to a busy day you recently had. A day that, maybe at the beginning, seemed like there was too much to handle. You had a long to-do list, but as you went through each hour of your day, you effortlessly checked things off the list. At the end of the day you looked back and realized you accomplished a great amount of responsibilities that day.

How did you spend your time that day? What did you

focus on? There was probably so much to get done that you didn't let distractions get in your way. A friend might have asked for some of your time, but you kindly told them you were too busy that day to do much. You chipped away at your list and each step of the way, you could feel the light at the end of the tunnel getting closer and closer. There was something that worked for you that day; think about how that day went and write down the details. This will be the outline of your "ideal busy day."

Now, let's look at times where maybe the day didn't go so well. You might have not even had as long of a to-do list as you did on your "ideal day." As the day went on, you got distracted. You didn't really have a list of priorities. Maybe the things on your list were of no interest to you, so you didn't really put the effort forth to get those things done. How were you spending time on that day?

Were you creating distractions? Were you hanging out with friends for lunch? Did your mom call you and you ended up talking on the phone for over an hour? Where was your focus?

Go ahead and write down a list of distractions that made this day less than productive. We will use this list later when we compare what we say yes and no to. Everybody has distractions. Some distractions we don't enjoy and don't always invite (like your mom calling you "just to talk"). Other distractions we might create or enjoy—movies, social media, friends, etc. Whether we invite these distractions or not, they are taking time away from us, when most of them can be controlled. Understanding when and when not to let distractions take over is key to time management.

2. Plan Your Week

I know planning your week seems like a pretty obvious and straightforward thing to do. If that's true, then how is it going for you so far? Saying that you just have a list of things that needs done in a day is one thing. Planning the day or week out in a specific order and scheduling your tasks changes the game completely.

Notice how this section is planning out your *week* and not planning out your *day*. This method can actually be done for both but planning out your week essentially gives you more freedom. You can plan some buffer time in case something doesn't go exactly as planned. Use these next methods to plan out an entire week, then repeat for each individual day.

If you are looking at a to-do list, would you say everything on that list is of equal importance? I can guarantee the answer is most likely "No." There must be at least one to three items that, if you do not get them done that day, could create a big problem. There are probably other items that can be held off until the next day, even if they are the easier choices.

When you look at a long list, what do you normally choose to do first? The easy task or the most important one? The easy one is the most common answer. What if you completed half the list, crossing off all the easy tasks, but in the end, didn't really accomplish anything important or of value? Have you done this before? If we let comfort or emotions decide how to tackle our day, we might not end up moving the needle as much as we would like.

The first easy step is to just list out all the responsibilities and items you need, should, or want to get done this week, in no specific order. Check your calendar, check your due dates on projects, days you need to be at work—all of it! This might look like a long list at first, but we are going to split it up to make it more manageable.

Now split this list into three categories: *Must* do, *should* do, and *want* to do. *Must* do would be days of work, school projects with a due date this week...anything that, if not done in time, would cause serious problems.

Starting with the *must* do, plan which days you should work on these items and when they are due. Notice I didn't say *want* to do these items. I know you *want* to work on your school project the day before or the day that it is due, but what if something goes wrong? I have had a few projects go wrong where my files didn't save to my flash drive correctly, or my printer died the day before an assignment was due. Talk about panic and chaos! Next, put your *should* do items on the days you think you could work on these.

Keep in mind how much time you plan to work on the *must* dos. If you have a big project that will take almost an entire day, or you have a long day of work on a certain day, don't add *should* dos to that day. You won't have enough time. Always leave time for variables.

After work, your normal fifteen-minute commute home could turn into an hour commute if there is an accident. Don't fill every single minute with something, as that's unrealistic anyway. Leave a little bit at the end of each time block.

Lastly, put the *want* to dos in the remaining spots. These are items that may be easy, but if you can't get to them, it is not the end of the world. Sometimes I even just keep these on a floating list by themselves. If I find extra time in a day and there is an easy one I can work on, I'll just quickly complete it and mark it off the list.

Plan Each Day

Now that you have your rough draft for the week, it's time to schedule out each day. The first and easiest thing to schedule will be anything that has already been scheduled for you—classes or work. You can't move these, so everything else needs to be planned around them.

Next, for each day, find the top one or two items that *must* get done that day. Estimate a time box for how long you should work on that item. If it's an item you plan to work on multiple times throughout the week, like a school project, plan out how much you'll be spending each day on that project. Once you know how much time is needed, ***schedule it!***

Things that are not scheduled are a lot harder to get done. It is easy for a distraction to slip in at 1:00 pm on Saturday if you do not have something planned *in writing* on your calendar. Think about it. If your friends have plans to go out at seven on Friday night, are you going to say yes to anything else for that time? No. That spot is already "claimed" or scheduled. If you do that with your important responsibilities, distractions won't make their way into that time block.

My entire life is planned around my calendar. I can easily forget when I have something planned. Before I say yes to anything, I check my calendar to make sure I have no prior obligations. Sometimes these obligations include meetings with other people, other times they are personal meetings, like ones I've attended regarding writing this book or creating content. Whatever it is, most of the time if it goes in the calendar, it is not changing and that time is blocked off.

Do this repeatedly for each day. Know what time is

already scheduled, add your *must* dos, then *should* dos, then *want* to dos. In the end, you will be looking at a good plan for your day. You should know roughly what you will be doing at each time of the day. When one "appointment" ends, instead of wandering around wondering what you should work on next, you'll have another time block with some responsibility attached to it.

I know you may be thinking this seems like overkill. Honestly, it may be a little over the top. I don't truly expect you to have every minute of every day planned. Although, listening to successful leaders, many of them claim having an entire day scheduled out is what helps them succeed in their business. The main part of this exercise is to look at your week *before* it happens instead of looking at your week *while* it happens.

Without a plan, it is very easy for time to slip away. As we said earlier, once time is spent, we can't get it back. However, a plan can help you adjust easier when stuff happens. What if you forgot about a responsibility, or you need to stay later at work? If you have a *must* do and something happens where you can't get it done at the time you thought you would, you can look at your plan for the week and adjust. Move the *must* do to later that day or week. You can track your timeline.

Let's say you have a plan to spend five hours on a

project spread out over five days. If you had an hour planned on Monday and something happened, you need to place that hour somewhere else, either later in the day or add it to the next day. It is easy to move an hour around here and there. What is not easy is planning to spend five hours the day before a project is due and have something come up that takes away half or all of the time you needed for it. Now you don't have room to adjust!

So, you might not have every minute of every day planned but having even a rough plan allows you to see into the future before it happens. It gives you room for adjustment. It also allows you to see where you have room to add more things and places where you can't allow any distractions.

3. Saying Yes vs. Saying No

This is something I wish I would have learned much earlier in life, as I have been a "yes man" for a large part of it. Some could say I still say yes to everything, but I have more control now than what I used to. I used to want to help everyone I could. If someone asked for help, I would almost always say yes unless I had something else more important planned. Even then, I would try to say yes, but at a different time.

The issue I found was, when I was saying yes to some things, I was actually saying no to a lot of other things. Things that could have added value to my life and helped me grow. I would say yes to a commitment a month or two out. It might be something small that was helping somebody else out. Small to me, but important to them.

A week or two later, I would find something that I wanted to go to. Something that would add value to me but was scheduled at the same time as the thing I already said yes to. Other times I would say yes to something knowing that it would add more pressure on to something else I was working on. I figured I was invincible and would find a way to make it work. I always made it work, but at the expense of getting burnt out and losing energy. No matter how strong you are, there is always a limit to what you can do. Stretching yourself too thin causes issues for you and others you are trying to help.

Lately, I have been thinking before just saying yes. I ask myself, "Is this in line with my goals for myself? Will this take away from something I am working on?" I'm not saying I only say yes if it benefits me. That is crossing the line of being selfish. I provide value where I can, but I want to make sure that I use my "yes" wisely.

Where does this come into play for you? Well, you now have a rough plan of what your week (or maybe your month) looks like. You can see how much free time you have available. You hopefully know what balance you need of fun versus work. Knowing all of this, I want you to use this whenever you're trying to decide whether or not to say yes to something.

I want you to learn and add value to others in as many places as you can. Saying yes to some opportunities can accomplish both of these at the same time. However, there is still a balance of fun and growth to strive for. I have been fully committed to growing myself as fast as I can, but I tend to forget to allow time to just enjoy myself and those around me. The other side of the coin is that you don't want to say yes to too many fun activities. By saying yes to too many fun, or *want* to do activities, you are saying no to activities that can help you grow as you near graduation.

Want your own time management chart? Get your bonuses at StudentSucessPrinciples.com

Summary

✓ We are all given the same number of hours in a day and week. How are you spending that time?

✓ Do a time audit. Look back and compare days where you had a great, productive day with days that weren't so productive.

✓ Plan out your day and week. Creating even a rough draft of what your week looks like allows you to adjust as the week progresses. Look at your week *before* it happens instead of looking at it *while* it happens.

✓ Balance your yes and no. Make sure before you say yes to something, you are not potentially saying no to something more important. Balance fun activities with ones that add value.

Morning Routine

"Some people dream of success, while other people get up every morning and make it happen"
-Wayne Huizenga

I am a strong believer that how you wake up every day greatly impacts how the rest of your day will be. I am sure you have heard of the expression "Someone woke up on the wrong side of the bed this morning!" When you quickly think about the phrase, you may ask, "How the heck does the side of the bed I wake up on matter?" This phrase is obviously not meant to be taken literally, but it refers to the attitude you are presenting to others.

Let me start by asking how a normal morning looks for you right now? Do you time out exactly how long it will take from the time you get out of your bed to out the door? Do you give yourself *just* enough time to wake up, get ready, and leave, just to get to your first class as it starts? Do you give yourself any time to think or plan out your day?

If you ask most people, especially those in high school or college, if they are a morning person, they will most likely give you a resounding "NO!" It is amazing how many people are dependent on caffeine to get themselves through their chaotic day. It amazes me how most people choose to start off a long day with a stressful and chaotic morning.

Think about it—if you know that you have a lot to do in a day, and are going to be busy all day, why would you start off your morning in a chaotic, out-of-control way? Wouldn't it be easier to start off with some control to your day, before potentially derailing the train from the tracks? Your mindset in the morning can drastically affect the rest of your day.

Think back to a morning where you were excited to get up. It might have been Christmas morning or a vacation. Maybe it was the morning of a job interview or the day of your senior prom. It is astonishing how easily you can get out of bed when you have a positive reason to do so. Why can't we create more positive reasons every day, rather than once in a great while?

If you are thinking to yourself, *I can never be a morning person!* I could tell you that you are right. If you think that way, you are absolutely correct, but what if I told you that you could become a morning person if you just adjusted a few things? Not only could you become a morning person, but you could also drastically increase your personal development level.

I know this is a bold statement, but hundreds of thousands of people have made the shift already. The international best-selling author Hal Elrod wrote a book back in 2012 that has changed the lives of many people, including myself, called *The Miracle Morning: The Not-So-Obvious Secret Guaranteed to Transform Your Life (Before 8am)*. Now, Hal likes to throw around the word *Miracle* more than others, but he is not far off.

While writing the book, he studied a vast number of high achievers to see what they did in order to succeed. One common theme he found from these superstars is that they all had some form of a morning routine. They woke up extra early in order to spend some alone time focusing on themselves and their day.

You see, Hal was in a very low spot in his life. One minute he was on top of the world as a high-end business coach making high six figures every year. In 2008 when the economy crashed, nearly all of his expensive clients "fired" him as a coach because they couldn't afford him. When he stopped and realized that he was living at rock bottom, he knew he had to change his life around and wanted to learn how to do it.

That is when Hal created the S.A.V.E.R.S.—a list of six different exercises that he put into a daily morning practice that completely flipped his life around. He took the six most used exercises from some of the most successful people in the world and created a routine that encompassed them all. After doing this, he was able to turn his life around in a few short months.

He was nice enough to write a book that covers these exercises in detail which I *highly* recommend you read. It is one book I re-read almost every year. I read it when I have challenges in my life because it reminds me how doing something so simple can really create successful results.

I will summarize the six exercises here, but Hal goes into more detail in his book as well as how to make the S.A.V.E.R.S. a daily habit.

S – Silence

The first *S* is for silence. Silence can mean different things for different people. For me it means meditation and appreciation. When I talk about meditation, many people think meditation is something only hippies do. There are many celebrities such as Tony Robbins, Katy Perry, Madonna, or Hugh Jackman that attribute their success to a daily meditation practice.

Meditation is really just clearing your mind from all of the distractions in the world. It's putting your body into complete relaxation, free from distractions. It means centering yourself before the start of a busy day.

There are plenty of guided meditations on YouTube or apps you can download, such as Headspace or Calm. They are usually just a recording of a calming voice helping you through breathing techniques and assisting you with clearing your mind. There are other types of meditations that you can do in the shower or on the way to school or work. They don't all involve sitting on a mat with your legs crossed.

Meditation takes practice, but with enough of it, you can really change the way your mind and body work. Take some time to research different guided meditations. It will take some practice to become good at it, but I promise it will be worth it.

A – Affirmations

I like to look at affirmations as a promise to yourself or a guide for who you want to be. There are some comedy skits out there of a man talking to himself in a mirror about how he is going to conquer the world, trying not to cry at his interview so he can land a job. That isn't necessarily the best way to do affirmations.

The better way to do affirmations is to imagine an end goal and write down what habit you are going to create (or a bad habit you want to eliminate) to accomplish that goal. For instance:

I am going to focus on making myself the healthiest version of myself. I am going to commit to going to the gym three days a week to make myself healthier.

By writing something like this down and reading it every day, the phrase will become a part of you who are. Some people think of affirmations as saying something as if it were already true.

I am the healthiest version of myself. I am completely healthy and comfortable with myself.

For one, your subconscious knows you are lying, so it is hard for you to believe the words that are coming out of your own mouth. Second, sometimes when you say something as if it has already happened, you are, to a degree, already experiencing a glimpse of that success. Your brain may see that glimpse as something that has happened, rather than something to chase after.

Think of some challenges and goals you have in your life. What are some things you would like to commit to? Write those down and read them every day. It might seem silly at first, but what if it actually worked? What if you started seeing a change in your behavior because every day, you remind yourself of who you want to become, and set yourself up for daily success rather than going through each day waiting for things to happen *to* you?

Affirmations also help you maintain a positive mindset. Have you ever woken up thinking the day was going to be bad, and the rest of the day was in fact bad? Your mindset had a lot of impact on how your day was going to turn out. Maybe you know someone who is frequently positive and good things always happen to them. Have you ever thought that their mindset may have something to do with the positive things that happen to them?

V – Visualization

Visualizations and affirmations are closely linked together. Visualizations are used by athletes all around the world. They use them to see a bunch of different outcomes before they actually happen. Then, when the situation presents itself, they have already lived out that moment many times in their head and were able to manifest it in their life.

If your goal is to get to the gym more often, visualize yourself at the gym. Visualize yourself putting in the hard work and seeing the results. This builds your motivation. Remember that results take a while to see, but now you have set a target of where you want to be.

I use visualizations when it comes to giving speeches. I visualize myself on top of large stages giving my best speech and seeing the audience react in a positive way. When the time comes to step up on stage, I have already seen myself in this scenario and know exactly how I want to execute my speech in order to achieve positive results.

Visualizations can also help build motivation. Once you see yourself in a certain situation and you can feel what it would be like to achieve that mission, you will want to work harder to reach that accomplishment. Get as detailed as you can in your visualization. Do not just generalize what it would be like to lose some weight or get good grades. Imagine all of the possibilities and how it would make you feel.

E – Exercise

For the non-morning people out there, I know the last thing you think of when you wake up in the morning is exercise. I get it, it takes all your energy just to get out of the bed. There is no way that you would be able to get up and do an entire workout in the early morning too.

What if exercise was the thing that could help you wake up in the morning? I am not saying you have to do a full workout; I just need you to get moving! Getting the blood flowing can really wake you up and get your brain pumping. If you work out later in the day, you know how great you feel about twenty minutes after your workout. You feel like you can take on the world! What if that started before you even left the house?

I don't do a crazy workout routine in the morning. I typically stretch with a combination of push-ups, sit-ups, and lunges. Nothing too strenuous, but it definitely gets my blood pumping and makes me breathe deep. If that isn't for you, you can look up five- or ten-minute yoga videos on YouTube. As long as you get your blood pumping, you are starting your morning off great.

Did I mention I don't drink caffeine in the morning? Due to the way I wake up, I have never been dependent on caffeine. When I say this to anyone, they typically look at me like I am an alien from outer space, but it's true! When I wake up with a purpose and get my blood flowing, I am ready to go for the day.

R – Reading

I know in school we have a lot of mandatory reading we must do. I hated reading almost every minute of every book in school. Then I discovered there is a whole world of books that I actually enjoy reading. I usually focus on personal development books. I like to learn from successful superstars. They put a lot of the things they have learned throughout their life into a book (just like this one). Why would I want to stumble and learn on my own when someone else spells everything out in black and white in a 200-page book?

Books are so easy to get your hands on now too. You can listen to them as an audiobook in the car on your way to school. You can download directly to your smartphone using the Kindle app or any eBook app. There is no excuse for not being able to read information that can help you grow.

If you have a certain hobby or interest outside of school or work, I can guarantee there are multiple books you can read on it. Exercise your brain in the morning! When I read for my ten to twenty minutes every morning, my brain ends up spinning with ideas on how I can better myself and my business.

Have you ever read a great article online and it inspired you to do something? Books can do the same thing. I stay far away from media. This is something you do NOT want to read first thing in the morning (trust me!). You could read fiction, as it can be something to enjoy in the morning before your day starts, but I would recommend personal development books. If you want to see a list of my favorite books, check out **www.SuccessAfterGraduation.com/books**. *The Miracle Morning* is on there, along with others that have really helped me get to where I am today.

S – Scribing

Hal needed a thesaurus for this one. Scribing is a fancy word for writing, but *W* wouldn't work well with a good acronym. Writing can be another great way to get your brain going. I admittingly don't do this enough and wish I did. This is something I continue to work on. I write a lot down in Evernote, which is an online app that stores notes in the cloud. I can create templates that I use daily or weekly for inspiration.

Write about wins for the day before. Write about things you want to improve on. Write about dreams you had overnight. Write about how you are feeling in the morning. It doesn't matter how great the grammar or spelling is because you'll be the only one reading it. It's fun to look back and see the experiences you've had! You don't have to write forever, but again, this is something that will get your brain up and running. Plus, it is time you are spending with yourself before the chaotic day begins.

Practicing the S.A.V.E.R.S.

The S.A.V.E.R.S. do not have to be done in any particular order. To begin, you may not be doing all six right away and that is okay. The fact that you are spending even ten minutes focusing on yourself instead of rushing around to get out the door can make a big difference.

I spend about 25-35 minutes on my miracle morning. I am out of my house by 6:00 am, so I have an alarm set for

4:45 am. It is hard to wake up much earlier than I already am. **Silence**, **Affirmations**, and **Visualizations** are easy. I clear my mind for a few minutes in **Silence**, I have five **Affirmations** written down that I read, and I **Visualize** how my day is going to go, and where I plan to be in a year.

With exercising I typically just do fifty sit-ups, push-ups, and lunges. This is enough to wake me up and cause a little bit of a sweat. After a shower and breakfast, I will try to squeeze in at least ten minutes of reading. If I don't have time for that, I listen to an audiobook or podcast in the car during my commute.

Writing might actually happen more towards the end of my day. Writing isn't my favorite, but I try to get it in when I can. That is the beauty of the S.A.V.E.R.S. though. It doesn't have to be perfect, there aren't any strict rules. The main focus of this routine is growing your personal development. Spending your entire morning rushing to get out of the door isn't going to grow any part of your life (other than your PR for fastest shower time!).

Ways to Wake Up Easier

Hal has a great foolproof strategy for getting yourself out of bed easier. Here are a couple of my tips to help with this:

1. **Use a loud alarm and put it across the room**

   Do you push your snooze multiple times? This makes getting up even more difficult. Falling asleep for five minutes at a time puts a huge strain on your body. Moving it across the room makes you move your body, helping you wake up.

2. **Turn some lights on**

   When you go to turn off your alarm, flip a bright light on. It is a lot harder to fall asleep with a bright light in your room. I have a geeky tech way of doing this. I have a smart outlet in my room. When I tell my Google Home "good morning," it flips on a table lamp that lights up the whole room. My wife doesn't appreciate it, but it does get us out of bed easier.

3. **Prepare the night before**

   Hal talks about this in greater detail, but here is the summary. Instead of going to bed at night thinking of how *little* amount of sleep you will be getting, think about how positive the next morning is going to be. If you go to bed with a positive attitude about the next morning, chances are you will wake up with a better attitude. I'm sure there are times where you've stayed up late but had something exciting the next morning going on and you had no issue waking up. There were probably other times where you were dreading getting up the next morning, even with the same amount of sleep, and when you woke up you felt like a zombie. Your brain is more powerful than you think.

Summary

✓ The way you start your morning can drastically affect the rest of your day. Wake up a little earlier than you do now and spend time with yourself. Start implementing the S.A.V.E.R.S. any way that you can. Creating even just one habit can really help start your day.

✓ If you are in high school, have your parents hold you accountable when it comes to your new wake-up time. If you are in college, use a roommate or friend for an accountability partner. Text them every morning when you wake up or have them text you.

Relationships

"Saying hello doesn't have an ROI,

It's about building relationships"
-Gary Vaynerchuk

Relationships are one of the most valuable things you can invest in. I know it sounds weird to use the word "invest" when talking about relationships but in this context, invest means "to put energy into." Relationships hold more power than people think. When I say relationships, you might just think of friendships, the people you hang out with to have fun. Friendships are definitely one type of relationship, but I don't like looking at relationships as something you *just* enjoy.

When I look at relationships, I think of them as your surrounding environment. Obviously, some relationships are stronger than others, but think about the current relationships you have with those around you. How do they affect your environment? Think about how they affect your everyday life. Think about *who* you may have become because of your close relationships. These relationships probably affect you more than you would think.

I feel most people take relationships for granted. There isn't really anything wrong with that, but what if we step back and actually analyze relationships as a valuable asset? Think of the benefits you have received from your current relationships. Think of the benefit you have provided others within your current relationships. Hopefully there is close to a mutual benefit there. What if you were to grow your current relationships or start creating more of them? What if you focused on growing deeper, meaningful relationships as you move forward with your life? I bet you could start growing yourself personally.

Successful business people and entrepreneurs put a lot of value in their business relationships. Some might even claim they wouldn't be where they are today if it weren't for the relationships they have built. You may have heard it is not *what* you know, it is *who* you know. As much as I'd like to hope it is better to have more knowledge than know more people, I have found over my years that having good relationships with the right people has greatly helped with my success.

I have a group of friends that are like close family. We are there for each other in every situation. We travel together and meet as often as we can. That helps my social life greatly and I appreciate everyone in my group. I also have professional relationships that have opened bigger doors for me. I get connected with professionals that are successful and willing to help me grow. If I was just sticking to my close group of friends, I wouldn't be able to make these new professional relationships.

I once heard a guest on a podcast mention why he invests so deeply in relationships. He said, "If I were to lose everything in my business and my money, I would still have a solid relationship with people that would help me rebuild." I would like to believe as humans we are, for the most part, supportive givers. We want to see others succeed. If we have the resources, and it won't cost us too much time or money, we have no problem sharing those resources with the people we trust and know.

Picking Your Relationships

New friendships are a funny thing, especially when you are younger. You find a random person and pretty much decide you like them enough to want to hang out with them for the foreseeable future. You don't quite *learn* how to make new friends, it kind of just *happens*.

At this point in your life I am sure you have had your fair share of relationships. Some good, some bad. Some great, some absolutely horrible. You might not be at "expert level," but you definitely have experience in the relationship department. Do you pay attention to who you let in your "circle?"

When did you start deciding who's allowed in and who's not? It probably happened from a bad experience where you found out that you shouldn't have let someone in. Maybe they hurt you in a way, or you just realized they brought out the worst in you. Either way, you now have a good sense of who you would like to make new friends with.

What if I told you that who you pick and spend the most time with may actually have a bigger effect on who you are than what you think? Studies have shown that you are the average of the five people you hang out with most. Have you ever caught yourself acting different with different groups of friends? You aren't being fake, but different personalities might make you act slightly different or cause you to say different things.

Energies are different when you hang around different people too. We all seem to have that one friend that seems to be negative about everything. An entire group can be having fun, but there is that one person that seems to suck the fun out of everything. They never seem to be entirely happy. When they are part of a group, do you notice yourself become slightly more negative too?

I want to help you build a super team of relationships. A group of people that will consistently add value to your life and raise you up. A group that you enjoy being around and would give all of your energy into helping each and every one of them. Think of the Avengers or Justice League...sure, they have issues sometimes, but they work well with each other and challenge each other in positive ways.

What if you actually sat down, focused, and evaluated your current relationships? What if you made adjustments to create the ideal group that will help you succeed as you grow? That is what we are going to do right now.

Take a sheet of paper and write down all the people you know closest to you. This should be people you see at least once a month. You can include best friends that may have moved away too. (If you still hold a strong relationship with someone that is far away, they will definitely be someone you want in your ideal group).

Next write down positive and negatives for each person. I know this may be weird. I don't want you really rating your friends, but what we are doing is starting to find common characteristics between the people that are closest to you, and those that may just be acquaintances. As you start writing these characteristics down, pay attention to the characteristics that bring you the most comfort, or the characteristics that maybe help improve who you are.

Just because a friend challenges you does not mean that they are bad. They may just be trying to bring out the best in you. I have a friend that constantly calls me out on things I say I am going to do when I don't follow through with them. Does she annoy me sometimes? Yes. But I am better because of her. Some of these traits might just have an emotional attachment to them, and that's great too. I don't expect you to build relationships based off of black and white data and numbers.

Now that you have the characteristics of these friends written down, look at what you have written down for the five or six people you spend the most time with. My guess is that there are some common traits. I would also bet that you have some of the same qualities as what you see in your friends. Groups of friends obviously have a mix of people. Some friends are better at some things than others, but on average you are all very much the same.

With this group of five to six people defined and their common characteristics, you should have a pretty good picture of what type of people you are hanging out with. Hopefully you're happy with this group of people and characteristics. There is a chance, however, that maybe on reflection, this is not exactly the type of people you want to be spending time with. Do the qualities of this group reflect the type of person you want to be several years from now? If the answer is no, unless you start looking for a different group of people, you won't be where you want to be in the future.

People can change if they want to. It takes a lot of hard

work to get there. If you need to change and want to, by using practices in this book, I know you will accomplish your goals. However, it is a lot easier to change one person than it is to change an entire group of people. On top of that, it is easier for a person to change the group they want to hang out with compared to changing an entire group of people they are trying to move away from.

If you are happy with your current "inner circle" of relationships, that's great! I'm sure there is also room for improvement. The great thing is you can have more than one group of friends. I have a group of "business" friends and a group of "social" friends. Both have their own set of qualities that affect me differently.

When I want to have a great time, I know the type of people I want to hang out with. When I want to be challenged to become a better version of myself, I have a different group of people I associate with. In fact, my business or professional relationships are with people who are more successful than me. Seeing them succeed makes me proud of them for one, but it also challenges me to be better.

If you don't have multiple types of relationships, start thinking of qualities that you would put into different categories. Once you have those categories figured out, start searching for people you get along with that have the traits you are looking for. I promise expanding your circle of influence will never hurt you. It will only help you grow into a better version of yourself!

Providing Value in Your Relationships

Now that we have a general idea of what some ideal relationships look like, let's look at what type of value is being created in these relationships. Any good relationship has value being added from both sides. If you were the only one providing value in a relationship, I highly doubt that relationship would last very long.

When you wrote down the qualities and characteristics of your current relationships, I'm sure a lot of those describe the value they provide you. As humans we all enjoy getting value from others, and there is nothing wrong with that as long as you provide value in return.

Now, this isn't a game where you compare who gives more value. That isn't what friendships and relationships are about. Can you imagine if people went through life keeping score of who did more favors for the other? "Hey Bill, remember last week when I picked up that milk from the store? You still owe me for that." That would be crazy!

On the other hand, if you don't direct focus to the value you are providing and seem to take a lot more than you give, it might get to the point that friends start to think or realize you are never really there for them. Have you ever had a friend that always seems to ask for small favors here or there but is never around when you need them? You don't want to be that person.

Hal Elrod, who I mentioned wrote *The Miracle Morning*, has an acronym when it comes to adding value for others in a relationship—S.A.V.E., which stands for "Selfishly Add Value Everyday." When you have great relationships, you actually get enjoyment out of helping others. Since I am a tech geek, I really enjoy helping friends when they have questions on tech gadgets. They of course thank me constantly, and my one friend usually repays me with some amazing food (which is one of my favorite forms of payments any day!).

The great thing about constantly adding value to everyone is if and when you finally need a small favor, your friends are *more* than happy to help you out. The same can be said for professional relationships. If you are known as the person who constantly provides value to a specific person or even a group of people, they look forward to the chance to be able to help you with something. In the business world, it is sometimes looked at as bartering. I don't like looking at favors as transactions, though. I just know that as I continue to add value, I am helping others grow, as I continue to grow myself.

Let's look back at the list you wrote down of your close relationships. You wrote down characteristics of what you think of them. Now let's write down some characteristics, positive and negative, you think your friends would write down about you. This may be a little harder since you're evaluating yourself. I don't like to write positively about myself because it feels like bragging. This self-evaluation will be good for you though. It may point out where you could be lacking in the value department. If you can't write a decent list of good traits about yourself from some of your closest friends, you may need their help.

Next time you talk to your friends, see if they can write down a list of positive and negative characteristics that describe you. Tell them you are working on building stronger relationships. You want to know what you do right and some things you could work on. They may describe some things you don't actually see in yourself. Don't be offended by any negatives. The whole point of this exercise is to make you a better person. If you don't know what you are doing wrong, how are you going to fix those?

Relationships are one of the most important, valuable assets we have in our lives. If you don't have a surplus of strong relationships it can affect you negatively in an emotional and professional way. Relationships can open doors to whole new opportunities you would never think of. One of my key focuses is to continually add new relationships and grow my current ones.

I am hoping after reading this chapter, I have opened your eyes to how valuable relationships truly are. Maybe you didn't need me to point that out because you see how strong and valuable your current relationships are. Even if that is true, I am hoping you'll direct some focus to building new relationships and think about the types of relationships you want in your future.

The world is filled with billions of people, and each possible connection could lead to something greater. The next time you meet someone that you seem to "click" with, think about where this relationship could lead and how much they could help you grow.

Summary

✓ Relationships are very valuable

✓ Write down common characteristics of your current group of friends

✓ Great relationships benefit everyone involved

✓ Push yourself to grow and add relationships

✓ Find people with characteristics you want to grow in yourself

Finances

Budgeting

"A budget is telling your money where to go,

Instead of wondering where it went"

- **Dave Ramsey**

One of the student success principles you will want to carry with you your entire life is budgeting. If you talk to anyone financially successful, I can almost guarantee you they will mention how they budget all of their money on a monthly basis. Before we dig into the technical details of budgeting, let me explain why budgeting is so important and where so many people fail by not budgeting their finances.

If you have a job, there are probably times where you are practicing a juggling act of handling your expenses between paychecks. I get it, only having $20 in your checking account four days before payday is not fun. It is even worse if you need gas in your car and food to last until payday. Has this ever happened to you? If so, hopefully it is not every month. Do you ever wonder where all of that money goes?

If you are not currently earning money or working, you

may be asking, "Why is budgeting important to me right now if I am not making any money?" Well here is the thing: When you finish school and become successful after graduation, chances are you are going to be making a pretty healthy income. If you are not smart about your money, you could end up with as much money as you do now—*nothing*. Or even worse, so far in debt you have to file for bankruptcy. So why not learn early, when there is less money to budget?

A Gallup poll shows that only one third of Americans actually budget on a monthly basis. If you are not sure of where your money is going, you are not alone. For most, every payday is like a small game. You start off with a "full" bank account and then slowly drain it as you throw it at multiple expenses. Some expenses may be required like insurance, gas, and groceries. Other expenses might not be so necessary like eating out, shopping, and games.

Unnecessary expenses are okay, but not if you spend too much of your money on them. I am sure there are some months when you have plenty of money left in your bank account before payday, and others where you are scraping by. This tells me that you are inconsistently spending money in different areas without realizing it. Or, maybe you *do* realize it, but aren't worried about it because you feel you *need* to spend it to have fun, or that expensive item was on sale and you just had to have it.

The problem is you pay for that splurge a few days later when you are out of money and do not get paid for a few more days. As humans, one of the largest causes of stress is finances. They say money doesn't buy happiness, but it does make life easier. Ever notice on payday you are usually stress-free, and as your bank account drains down to nothing, your stress starts climbing? What if you could control that and win this never-ending game of money management?

What if I told you that budgeting was something simple you could do that would lower your stress, and maybe even put more money in your pocket for things you want in the future? If you read the book *The Millionaire Next Door* or Chris Hogan's book *The Everyday Millionaire* you will see countless examples of millionaires that live in every corner of the country growing up with very simple, average-income lives.

One of the major keys to their success is budgeting. They know where every dollar they spend goes every month. They control their money rather than let their money control them. They control which areas of their lives receive the most "attention" with their money. When many people hear *millionaire*, they assume that means they are making well into six figures a year. That is not always true. There are plenty of people making less than $100,000 a year, but after investing for twenty to thirty years, are able to reach the millionaire mark. They know how to save, invest, and budget their money.

Budgeting simply means having every dollar of your monthly paycheck allotted or spent, before you physically spend it yourself. Imagine if you knew when you received your paycheck that you would spend exactly $100 on food and $50 on entertainment. You would have a number for every area that you spend money on, and you would be happy with each number. One of those areas would hopefully be savings or investments. You would know how much money you would have left all the way up until your next paycheck. Hopefully you are nodding your head yes right now.

When people hear the word *budget*, they instantly think of how hard and how much math it will take to achieve this. They think it involves endless hours sitting down with a calculator, crunching numbers, attempting to figure everything out. What if your budget only took fifteen minutes a month? What if that fifteen minutes could save you a bunch of money? Fifteen minutes can save you more than a bunch of money on car insurance!

Get a Checking Account

Let me make a small side note here. In order to get the full value from any online budgeting app, you will need to have a bank account set up with an online banking login. If you do not have a bank account, the first step will be to open one.

If you are under eighteen, you will need your parents to come with you in order to open one. If you just convert your paycheck to cash every time, it will be very difficult to track your money. I have also found it is easier to have an electronic view of your money compared to having to always recount your cash left in your sock drawer.

As you start earning more money and want to shop online, a debit card will be a must. As technology grows, there are places starting to go cashless. When applying for apartments or mortgages in the future, they will need proof of how much money you have saved in your checking and savings accounts. It is very difficult to make any large financial decisions without a checking account, so I highly recommend opening one if you do not currently have one.

Auditing Your Life

In order to get started budgeting, the first thing you are going to have to do is audit all of your expenses. This is going to be an easy, but potentially eye-opening task. There are many students who realize how much they spend on unnecessary areas and get upset about the money they are wasting.

The good thing is, all of that is about to change. One of

my favorite apps to help with budgeting is mint.com. This was created by Intuit and it will give you a deep-level view of how much money you are spending in each area of your life.

To get started, go to mint.com and sign up. Once you open an account, it will guide you to connect your bank account. This isn't so they can charge you for anything, this is so they can do a deep dive on your finances. Search for your bank and type in your login you would use to log in to your online banking. After you do this, all of your transactions will be imported and categorized. This app does a pretty good job of knowing how to categorize each transaction. For instance, it will put Walmart under groceries, any gas station under a "fuel/gas" category, etc. Sometimes it won't know how to categorize a transaction, so may pick a wrong one. Do your best to take a quick look and make sure all categories make sense.

After this, you can generate some reports to see how all of these categories stack up. When I did this for the first time, I realized I was spending *way* too much money on fast food and restaurants. I realized where all of my money was going— into my stomach! You can even dive down into specific restaurants or stores. You'll start to see that $3 cup of Starbucks every day really adds up quick.

Creating Your New Budget

Once you realize where all of your money is going, it is time to change things up so you can plan where it will go, rather than trying to see where it went. Mint allows you to create a budget by listing out different categories and how much you want to spend in each of those categories. The first thing you need to do is put in your income. Without that, it is impossible to know how much you want to spend in each category. If your income fluctuates each month because your schedule is inconsistent, put in an average, or a number that is on the lower end. In other words, stay on the conservative side. Putting your best paycheck in for a regular income won't help anyone.

Once you have your income in, add the categories that *have* to come out each month. If you have a car, you'll need to include insurance, gas, and maybe even a car payment. The great thing is, Mint will now tell you how much you spend on gas every month, so you already know what to budget for gas. Your car payment and insurance should be consistent every month. Go through and add any other bills that you have to pay every month, like a cell phone if you pay for that on your own.

Once all of your *must* do expenses are added, Mint will tell you how much money you have left to budget for the month. Unfortunately, many times this is a lot less than we would like. But isn't it nice knowing ahead of time how much is left? Knowing what money is coming out before it happens is like seeing into the future. There are so many times I hear stories of students forgetting about that $15 Netflix bill that comes out a day before their paycheck, and spending money as if that $15 isn't going to disappear.

Surprises may be great when you get something you want but forgetting that a bill or transaction is coming out of your account is not a surprise I like to deal with. Having every expected expense laid out in your budget should leave almost no surprises. You should also make sure you know when all of your due dates are for any bills you may have. I try to get my due dates as close to paydays as possible. If your due dates land on inconvenient dates, most times you can call and have those moved up a few days.

Looking at how much money you have left after your *must* do expenses are paid, you can now control where that money is going to be spent. What's nice is you have complete freedom on how this money is spent! If you really like eating out, then put a larger percentage of your budget towards that. Make sure you keep your numbers realistic because once you set this, you are creating a commitment.

You shouldn't create a $20 food budget if you have been spending hundreds a month on food in the past. Yes, it would be great to only spend $20 on food to save money, but unless you have extreme discipline, you are going to go over, which will then take away from another budget item.

Your first few months of your budget are not going to be perfect. You are going to overspend in some areas. Budget items will need to be adjusted and that is okay. This is a learning process. You should still do your best to stick to your budget. If you are down to the last twenty dollars on your shopping budget, you should not be going to the mall. I don't know any trip to the mall that costs less than twenty dollars unless all you do is window shop.

I keep a constant eye on my budget. I want to know how I am doing at all times. Mint will consistently update with each transaction you create. It will then let you know how much money is left in your budget. No math for you to do! I also keep a constant eye on my bank account. If I am following my budget, my bank account should match. I still like to keep track of how much money is left compared to how many days are left until next pay. If my bank account is dropping fast and I still have several days until my next paycheck, my lifestyle will change to match. I will have to say no to going out for drinks with friends because I do not want to dip into another budget I have allotted.

Now, I know I said this would take only fifteen minutes. The first few times you work on your budget may take a little more than that, especially the initial setup. After a few months though, your budget shouldn't be changing too much, so you can just copy the budget from one month to the next. Mint already does this for you. Make sure you pay attention to any expenses that are specific to a month.

For instance, you probably get an oil change every few months. Keep that in mind for the months that it will be due. Also pay attention to annual subscriptions. Every January my Amazon Prime account renews for $120. I have to make sure I increase my shopping budget for January and then lower another budget category for the month.

Again, I do not expect your budget to be perfect. It is difficult to remember every expense that may come up, and surprises do happen, but controlling as much as you can still makes a big difference. If you remember, I also mentioned where you may be able to save money. When I realized how much money I was spending on eating out, I immediately cut back on those expenses. That gave me an extra $50 - $100 a month extra back in my pocket that I could put into savings for a future time.

If you find an area that you are spending a lot of money in and want to lower it, you too can save a lot of money. I highly suggest putting that money towards any debt you may have. If you have a car payment, paying extra on it will only help you pay it off sooner. Paying on debt is a whole other conversation. Just know that any extra money you can save from a budget area can be moved and paid extra on any debts.

Hopefully after reading this chapter you realize how budgeting can really help you get a handle on your finances. Handling finances might even seem easier now if you do not have as much money to manage. It is a great idea to start the practice now, so when you start making a comfortable income, you can handle that extra money like a pro.

I don't want you to do what I did, which was go out and buy a brand-new car and throw all my money at eating out. It is crazy to think you can get such a large increase in income and not really have extra money left over after a paycheck. Sticking to a budget may feel like sticking to a diet. It is not the easiest thing in the world but knowing how it can drastically help you now and forever in the future should be a big motivation to stick with it. If you don't, chances are you can rack up some credit card bills or end up with no money left days before you get paid again.

Learn from my experiences and many others' before you. If you don't have a strong handle on your money, things can spiral very quickly. Doing something as simple as a budget can give you the upper hand on your financial future. I am also a strong believer that if a large number of millionaires have a monthly budget, they must be doing something right.

Summary

✓ Get a checking account
✓ Audit your current expenses
✓ Use an online app to create a monthly budget
✓ Your budget will change, but stick with it!

Money Management

"Making more money will not solve your cash problems if cash flow management is your problem"

- Robert Kiyosaki

The previous chapter covered budgeting in detail. I think budgeting needs a full overview in order for you to understand what it takes to manage your money before you spend it. Budgeting has been attributed to the number one success of people who are financially free, which is why I wanted to dive deep into it.

The following chapter could easily be broken into several individual chapters, but this book isn't a finance book. It is a book on principles that will help you succeed after graduation. This chapter is going to be a list of dos and don'ts that I have personally learned along the way. Some of these tips come directly from Dave Ramsey, the number one personality for helping families get out of debt and financially free.

If you want to learn more detail on the things I am covering in this chapter, you can spend some time on DaveRamsey.com, or search around google for a deeper-level explanation. If I went into the numbers, some readers' eyes would gloss over and they wouldn't be able to absorb the main points I am trying to make. As you move your way through the Internet, it is almost guaranteed that you'll discover conflicting viewpoints, which is perfectly okay.

My main concern is you may not have heard or know about any of the areas of money management I will be covering. I do not want you to make the same mistakes I made. I want you to *learn* from mistakes and learn the tips that have helped me pay off nearly all of my debt, other than my house. There is no point in you succeeding after graduation and landing a job you love if you can't manage the increase in income that comes along with it.

Before we get into the keys to financial freedom, let me explain what financial freedom means. Right now, money is something that makes your "world go around." You keep a constant eye on your checking account and almost every transaction (hopefully) is tracked and thought about before you spend your preciously-earned money.

Your life is controlled by how much money is in your bank account and how many bills you owe. Financial freedom basically means you have enough assets, or items, that hold positive value that you don't have to worry about making a specific monthly income in order to live a certain lifestyle. In some eyes this may just seem like the word *rich*, but it is much more than that. Imagine having such a handle on money that your bills take up an extremely low amount of your monthly expenses! Imagine that when you go to a restaurant, you don't have to worry about the prices on the menu because you know you have more than enough in the bank! What if I told you financial freedom isn't solely dependent on the amount of money you make, but also is created by the way you *manage* your money? In fact, there are many people in the world who make a great income, but because of mismanagement, are nowhere close to financial freedom.

Financial freedom is usually the ultimate goal. Once you hit that "status," there is usually a lot less stress because you get to spend your energy on things you enjoy, rather than worrying about where your next paycheck will be coming from. If you follow these money management lessons laid out below, it will make everything a lot clearer, and hopefully get you to where you want to be sooner.

Let's get started.

Emergency Fund

According to a CNBC article from 2018, only 39% of Americans have enough money to cover a $1,000 emergency[4]. Now I'm sure right now, $1,000 seems like a lot of money and it would be difficult to cover an emergency of that size. Hopefully right now, short of a medical emergency, you don't have anything going on in your life that would create an emergency that expensive.

As you get older and buy a house, thousand-dollar emergencies have a higher chance of coming up, because you have expensive assets in your home that could break, or a car that could need an expensive repair. Anytime you have to cover an expensive emergency, you take many steps back on your journey to financial freedom.

Emergency funds create a sense of security. Imagine how you'd feel if you know that under most circumstances, anything that breaks could be covered easily without having to run around to find the money? We already talked about how bad debt can become...covering an emergency with a credit card should *not* be the answer.

As I write this chapter, I have had two small emergencies happen within the last year. Last winter, our furnace broke in the middle of the first snow that has happened in Charleston in over five years. The temperature in the house was getting down into the fifties so I had to bring out a repairman to fix the furnace.

After he took a look, the quote was $400. That $400 can cover a lot of groceries or shopping. This was towards the end of the month and my budget for the month did not include a random $400 expense. Luckily, I had the money in my emergency fund and was able to pay him cash without worrying about it. Over the next month or two, I slowly replenished the emergency fund. In the past, I would have had to charge it and spend several months to pay it off, which would have probably meant a total cost of almost $500 for a simple furnace repair.

Just recently I took my car in for an oil change. While it was at the shop, they noticed my tire tread was really low. They recommended I get new tires if I was planning to go on any long trips soon. Well, they caught me one week before a 700-mile trip to Ohio. The cost was $800 for three new tires. Ouch!

Again, luckily, I had the money in my emergency fund. Trust me, I do not enjoy spending $800 on tires, but it sure feels a lot better than not having the money and having to use a credit card. I paid using my debit card that day, and don't have to worry about those tires anymore. I will have a nice, safe trip with my family up to Ohio with no thought of future payments on a set of tires.

In the beginning, saving up for an emergency fund is not going to be fun. Saving $50 or more a paycheck and putting it away for a rainy day goes against our wants. We want to spend that money on ourselves, not put it aside so we may or may not use it in the future. I promise you, there will be a time where you will use that emergency fund, and you will be thanking yourself over and over.

The ultimate goal is to save three to six months of expenses. Once you have a budget in place, you'll know exactly what those expenses add up to. And once you are debt-free, which you'll read about below, you'll have plenty of money left over to save up that emergency fund and create a great sense of security for yourself.

Make sure your emergency fund is separate from all of your other money, but in a place that you can easily access within a day. My emergency fund is in a separate bank account with a separate bank. I can't "accidentally" use my emergency fund on something that is not an actual emergency.

Dump the Debt

Debt is one of the most socially acceptable issues people have today. "Everyone" has debt, so if I have it, it does not seem to be that big of a deal. Well, if you study millionaires (which I am assuming you would love to be one), you would realize that very few of them have debt, and if they do, it is a very small percentage of their net worth. Debt is the gift that keeps on taking. In Proverbs 22:7 it is stated that "The borrower is slave to the lender." Think about it. Every time you get paid, the first question is, "Which bills are due in the next two weeks?"

When we owe money to a bank for the money that we borrowed, we are forever a slave to them until (**if**) we pay off the loan. As if being stuck in monthly payments weren't bad enough, we are paying *interest* mixed in with the payment. When interest is working against you, you are literally throwing money away with every payment you make. A good percentage of our payments are going directly into the bank's hands instead of paying down the balance of the loan. Would you go to the grocery store and pay $200 for $175 worth of groceries? That is essentially what you are doing with your monthly payment.

The worst type of loan to get, which 70 percent of car buyers have today, is auto loan debt. We already talked about the interest that you pay, but as you continue to pay month to month on your car, your car is *losing value*. On a multi-year loan, there is a point in time where you have eventually paid more on the loan than what the car is worth, and since you are slave to the lender, you have to continue to pay until the balance of the loan is gone.

Here are some simple numbers to show you what it costs to buy a brand-new $31,000 car over five years at a 2.5% interest rate.

Total amount paid over 5 years:	**$33,010**
The car is now worth:	**$11,629**
Total loss in value of:	**$21,381**

You are losing over $350 a month!! Do you really think you can afford that car now?

Now, new cars are obviously a lot worse than used cars. Used cars will not be nearly as dramatic. They are also a little easier to pay cash for. Paying cash for a car sounds ridiculous, I know. Only rich people can do that, right? Wrong! Rich people do pay cash, but they are also rich for a reason. Buying your first car with cash might seem pretty intimidating but it is definitely possible. You will most likely not be able to pay cash for a high-end used car, but working your way up to that nice car is not too difficult.

You will have to start off with a lower-valued car (say

four or five thousand dollars). The great thing about this is the value does not depreciate very much, since all the value has already been taken out. You are basically just parking your $5,000 in a car so you can use it later when you have more cash to upgrade.

Over the next year you can save $300 (or more) a month, which is about the amount you may be willing to pay for an actual car payment, but this $300 a month does not have interest hidden in it, so you are getting the full value out of the $300. At the end of the year you'll have an extra $3,600 to throw on top of your $5,000 car and will be able to purchase an $8,000 car if you so desire. You can continue to keep upgrading until you have your $15,000+ car. This may take several years, but when you have this, you will no longer have interest-filled payments to pay while your car is *losing* value. You can then use the money you are saving on payments and interest and invest it in something that actually pays back money rather than takes away from you through interest. This leads us to the magic of compound interest.

When I started my first job out of college, within a month I felt I "deserved" to get a brand-new car right off the lot. It was a nice Hyundai Sonata, with heated seats, backup camera—everything I could dream of! I spent just over $20,000 on it. At the time, I was driving over 600 miles a week back and forth to work. Two years later, it was worth around $11,000 while I still owed about $18,000. I was driving around a car that was worth almost half of what I owed.

It took me a while to make extra payments in order to get the principal down to a number where I was able to trade it in. Banks will not give you a loan for a car if it is worth way less than the loan price. That would be like you giving a $500 loan to a friend who lets you use their iPad. If they don't pay you, you're stuck with a used iPad worth about $250. Would you make that deal?

Having a laundry list of payments to different banks or lenders is not a great way to manage your money. Just because you can afford the payments doesn't mean you can afford the purchase. The money you lose in interest to the bank, combined with the loss of interest you could be *gaining* from an investment, makes it extremely difficult to achieve a financially free status. Paying cash will always help you out in the long run. If you don't have payments, it's impossible for that asset to be seized due to nonpayment. The main payments you should have in your life are taxes, insurance, and a house payment.

The Magic of Compound Interest

Compound interest is the magical wealth-building tool only the rich seem to know about. What if I told you there was a way to make money without having to do much at all?

You can actually make money while you sleep (and dream of dollar bills jumping over a fence into your wallet). I am not talking about some illegal Ponzi scheme. I am talking about using compound interest as a tool to earn your money for you.

Have you ever wondered how someone only making $50,000 a year can become a millionaire? I promise it is not because they are doing something illegal (although that is how it played out in the show *Breaking Bad*!). They are living below their means and investing all of their extra money into accounts that provide a profit on their investment. Over time, this continues to exponentially grow and make this median income family's net worth well above the national average. This is all due to the great magic (math) of compound interest.

Compound interest is the money a bank, or an investment account, pays you for leaving your money in their account. When invested in stocks, the interest is the value gained on the money you gave them to invest in their company. What's great is since your account can grow from the interest, even if you do not add any money to it, the account can grow by itself! $1,000 invested at 5% interest is worth $1,050 after a year; the $1,050 invested is then worth $1,102 at the end of the second year. Your $1,000 original investment has increased over $100 in just two years. Imagine how the math works when you work with larger numbers!

Most of us seem to pour our money into unneeded things like our morning coffee trips and big shiny toys. We may even use debt to accomplish this. What we do not realize is that these "needs" are costing us more than the sticker price. It seems so simple and innocent to spend three dollars here and there on small purchases like coffee or fast food runs. What we don't realize is that over time, these purchases can add up. Not only can they add up, but if you invested the money from these into a money market account that earns compound interest, it is even more expensive than you may first realize.

Let's say you buy your $3 coffee five days a week. Over the year that adds up to $780. Over five years that is almost $4,000. That doesn't seem too bad, right? Well $780 a year invested in a good mutual fund earning 10% a year over five years is worth over **$5,200.** That hurts a little more now, doesn't it? That is only a $3 coffee (which is probably if you get a discount, as most coffee costs more).

As you can see, compound interest works for you and is a huge key to financial freedom. The more money you have to save away in an interest earning account, the better. Also, compound interest only gets better with time. The earlier you can invest the better off you'll be. The hard part about investing is, in today's world, we are used to instant gratification.

With social media, the minute you post something you can get instant feedback. If you want to buy something, open your smartphone and tap *Buy*. Compound interest does take a while to take off, but I would much rather make small sacrifices now if I know it will pay off exponentially in the future.

Interest can also hurt you. This is a bit of a reflection back on debt. Banks love interest when it is in their favor. You can get an auto loan for $8,000, but if you pay the minimum payment on that for five years, the total you'll pay for that is about $8,800. That is, if you get a good interest rate. When you look at the interest on a credit card, which can be upwards of 25%, by paying a minimum payment of $25 on an $800 balance, you will end up spending over $1,300 to pay it off. That's over $500 in interest just for borrowing a small amount of $800. Most people borrow way more.

My point is, interest can work very much in your favor. The more you invest and let compound interest work for you, the more money you will have, and the quicker you will move towards financial freedom. I know people who can live their lifestyle solely on the interest they make from their investments.

Ten percent interest on a million-dollar investment pays out $100,000 a year. That sounds pretty good for just putting money away in a bank. I know it will take a while to get to that point, but compound interest can make it happen. A one-time $60,000 invested at 10% will yield one million dollars at the end of thirty years. That is, if you add nothing to it. That is some crazy math!

Moving Out

Usually the first step after graduation will be moving out on your own or with friends. You may have already moved out during college if you are living near a campus away from home. Either way, moving out is a big step that comes with a lot of responsibilities, both financially and personally.

I moved out when I was twenty-years-old. I had my son and wanted to get a place of my own. With some luck I was able to find a condo in foreclosure to purchase, and was fortunate enough to get some help from my parents in the beginning. They helped because they knew I was working very hard to balance being a dad, going to school, and working all at the same time. I was also paying my own way for college, so they pitched in a little each month.

Rent, Don't Buy

The number one thing I learned was that moving out is definitely more expensive than you would think. I am a math nerd and I tried running all of the numbers before moving out. There always seems to be extra expenses you don't think about, especially when you buy.

Moving out seems like a rite of passage. When you get that first job, I'm sure moving out will be at the top of your list of things you want to do. Before you do that, you want to pay very close attention to your finances. Whatever you think you can afford, I would recommend cutting it by at least 20%. Food costs, your social life, and other expenses you don't think about will quickly find their way into your life.

I would also not recommend buying a place, even if it seems like a great deal. When you own a place, you are in charge of fixing *everything*. Anything that breaks, you have to cover. Hot water tanks, HVAC systems, and roofs are all very expensive to fix. Insurance and taxes are also an expense you have to worry about with buying. Yes, you can technically start building value and equity in a house, but in the beginning, chances are it is going to be very expensive. You don't start making money back on a house until after four or more years. Who knows where your life will be in the next four years? Your job or family could drastically change, causing you to move somewhere else and possibly lose money on a house.

Renting is convenient because most of your expenses are fixed. Rent may go up from year to year, but all repairs are covered by the landlord. You typically get access to nice amenities too like a pool, fitness center, or walking trails. The monthly payment might seem similar to buying, but again you are not on the hook for repairs.

Your biggest goal in the beginning should be living as inexpensive as possible, especially if you have student loans hanging over your head. Imagine living like a college student on a full-time salary. You would have a lot of extra money left over to pay extra on your debt, or to put away for savings or investments. You have so much time before you have to worry about buying that "dream house" so there is no reason to rush.

Another way you can save money is moving in with another roommate or two. Maybe you had a bad experience with a roommate in school, but after graduation you have the chance to move in with another young professional. You won't have to worry about someone not paying rent or disrespecting the house. If you are going to move in with a roommate, make sure they have a solid full-time job, and you both share the same values of what you want your living space to be like.

Currently, I am very happy with where I ended up as far as moving out and the house I live in, but I can't help but think where I'd be and how much money I could have saved if I didn't jump into a mortgage halfway through college. Try to make your decisions using logic and calculations, not emotions. Emotions can get you in trouble. Once you sign a lease or a mortgage, it is not easy to get out.

Being Smart with Money

As you can see, I have learned a lot about money in my short life after graduation. I know I have plenty more to learn too. I always try to pay attention to what principles other successful leaders are practicing, and I have very large goals for my future. Money is not everything in the world, but it does contribute a lot to the lifestyle we lead.

Learning to be smart with money early will pay off exponentially in the future. You do not want to look back in five years and see a trail of dumb mistakes. I'm sure you'll make plenty of them, but make sure you learn from them. For me, the biggest thing is keeping attention and focus on how you are managing your money. If you do not pay attention to it, your money will slip away and you will always be chasing ways to replace it. Put yourself in a position where managing money comes easy and you get to enjoy the life that comes with it!

Summary

✓ Lower your debt as much as possible – It is expensive!

✓ Having an emergency fund gives you some security. It also lowers the risk to use a credit card for an emergency

✓ Compound interest can work for you and earn you money while you sleep.

✓ Make smart decisions with money. Don't let emotions control what you do with your money

Adulting

Getting into College

"Nothing is better than reading and gaining

More and more knowledge"

- **Stephen Hawking**

Success after graduation can mean different things to different people. If you are looking for success after *high school* graduation, getting into college is typically at the top of the list. Let me start by saying I strongly believe that you do not have to college in order to succeed after graduation, but in many cases it helps. What I am trying to say more is just because everyone says you should go to college does not mean you have to. If college isn't 100% for you, then you can skip this chapter. If you are debating on whether or not you should go to college and are unsure of what it takes to get into one, this chapter is definitely for you.

Getting into college may not be the easiest thing, but the principles to get in are simple. By simple I mean they aren't a major secret, but there are some principles that will get you in and help you do better in college than if you didn't know them. I will lay those out in this chapter.

The FAFSA

FAFSA stands for Free Application for Federal Student Aid. This is an application created by the government to gauge how much financial aid they are willing to give a student based on the income of their parents. Unfortunately, this doesn't consider that parents may not always be the people paying for the student's college.

I personally paid for my entire five years of college. My parents did help with some living expenses, but for the most part the bill was 100% on me. I learned a lot from paying for my college and can completely understand why my parents weren't able to help me through school. I can also say I am debt-free after paying off the $15,000 I collected through school, and I am better because of it.

One thing I always engrain into every student I talk to is how important the FAFSA is. First of all, it is a free application that can only result in free money. Where else can you fill out a piece of paper with the possibility of receiving thousands of dollars? Any money received from the government is one hundred percent yours for education and doesn't have to be paid back.

The reason why I pound this information into students' (and parents') heads is there are way too many families that do not fill it out. Why, I don't know. Sometimes it is because of confusion with the application or lack of knowledge or misunderstanding of how much money they can get. According to NerdWallet, in 2018, $2.6 BILLION went unclaimed by graduates[5]. This was by 661,000 students that didn't fill out the FAFSA and would have been eligible for the Federal Pell Grant.

The Pell Grant goes to lower-income families and can be renewed for up to six years with an average amount of almost $4,000. I would be interested to see how many of those students ended up not going to college because of the expense. That $4,000 could have been the difference between them going to college or not!

One other reason families do not fill out the FAFSA is because they are afraid of their legal status. Luckily, as of the writing of this book, students can be labeled as an "eligible non-citizen." Meaning that even if a student's parents are not legal U.S. residents, the student can still receive federal aid. A simple google search of "FAFSA and legal status" will return results on how to fill out the FAFSA if this applies to you.

One final note on the FAFSA. There are different ".com" websites out there that will try to charge you to fill out the application for you. You should NOT have to pay for the application (hence the first word of the acronym, "Free"). Make sure when you go to fill it out you go to *fafsa.gov* and follow the easy instructions. The application is mostly dependent on parental information, so make sure you have all tax information for the last few years available in order to accurately fill it out.

The College Application

To get into almost any college, you are going to have to fill out a college application. Most are not too complicated, but some can take some time. They also typically cost money, which means you should choose wisely before applying to every college you can think of, hoping to get some acceptance letters back.

Deadlines are the most important thing to pay attention to. Each college you are interested in may have a different deadline. Early application openings can start as early as November...that's only a few months into your senior year! Which also means you will have to have all the information ready and college visits done before you start your senior year.

Each college has a different level of complexity when it comes to their applications. Some are just a simple one- or two-page application, while others require a multi-page essay.

Unfortunately, if you weren't a fan of writing essays in high school, you are going to have to get good at writing to apply to different colleges. The one positive about these essays is you have a little more freedom when it comes to content. The essays are usually asking you to talk about your life and why you want to go to the school, or why you deserve to go to the school. Instead of getting a letter grade for a good essay, you have the ability to get accepted into college!

These essays are not something you can write up the night before they are due. If you are serious about applying and getting into a higher-level college, the essay is going to take some time and energy. If you are having issues writing, there are plenty of coaches out there that will help you write your essay. When searching for a writing coach, make sure they have plenty of testimonials and experience helping students get into the specific schools you are applying to.

One great website you can look at is https://www.commonapp.org. This site allows you to fill out one application and use it to apply to over 800 colleges that accept the application. You will notice as you start filling out applications, a lot of the colleges are asking for very similar information. The Common App makes it so you only have to fill out the application once so you don't have to keep refilling out the same information. Before you sign up, check and make sure multiple colleges on your list accept the Common App application.

Scholarships

I could honestly write an entire chapter on scholarships. Scholarships are the key to graduating with little to no debt. With billions of dollars up for grabs, there are plenty of opportunities to earn/win scholarships to help cover the cost of college.

Currently the U.S. has over $1.5 trillion in student loan debt, with the average student owing over $35,000. That is a lot of money. That money could be a great down payment on a house or provide you the opportunity to buy a real nice car in cash!

One thing I have noticed going through school is student loan debt seems to be 100% understandable/acceptable when talking about personal debt. There are different kinds of "bad" debt out there like credit card debt or car debt. Most people just accept student loan debt as a "necessary debt" in order to get a good education. The problem is, graduates are paying on this debt for over twenty or thirty years. You could technically pay off a house before you get student loans paid off! These monthly payments are holding graduates back from accumulating wealth.

I could get into a whole conversation about how school

should be more affordable, or how government help would be great, but as of this writing, that is not an option. So, where does that leave students? If they are part of a family who has the money to completely pay for college, that is great. Unfortunately, that is not the case for most families.

Most students must figure out how much money they will need to take out in student loans in order to attend college. The stress of paying those off will come later after graduation. Because everyone seems to have student loan debt and it is "acceptable," many students are not warned about how stressful the payments can be after they graduate.

Six months after graduation, payments kick in. In some cases, these payments can be well over $500 a month. For $500 a month, you could own a luxury car! If a graduate doesn't land a high-paying job after graduation, payments can be based off of income which land around $100 a month. That $100 a month doesn't even cover the interest, meaning that instead of paying the loan down each month, the loan amount actually *increases!*

This is where scholarships can become the key to helping graduate with the least amount of debt as possible. Scholarships are *free* money awarded to students to help pay for college. You can earn these in high school all the way through college graduation. Some scholarships come from the colleges themselves or from private donors. The key is finding these scholarships and applying to them.

Where to Find Scholarships

The most popular time students search for scholarships is their senior year of high school. This is also where most private donors like to gift their money. With college less than a year away, students should be working hard to find as many scholarships as possible. Where are the best places to look for scholarships?

School guidance counselors have great connections to scholarship donors and organizations. Donors can approach schools and set up a scholarship fund for students from a specific school. They can also make scholarships available to entire cities or counties. Your school counselor should have the inside scoop to a lot of these scholarships available in your local community. A goal of yours should be to visit your school counselor once a week, or at least every other week. If your counselor doesn't know you on a first-name basis, you are not going often enough.

In some cases, counselors get the honor of choosing students for awarded scholarships. I was able to earn a $500 scholarship from my counselor because she knew I fit the criteria, and she knew how hard I was working to earn scholarships. I also noticed that when she found out about scholarships I was eligible for, she would forward them to me, or give me the application the next time I saw her. This took very little effort; all I had to do was build a relationship with my counselor and she wanted to help me succeed.

There are also a great number of websites specifically built for scholarships. They are like google search engines that help narrow down your search based on grades, demographics, major, and more. Some of my favorite are Scholarships.com, Cappex.com and Scholarly.com.

The best part about these scholarship sites is after you sign up and fill out a profile, they will email you a tailored list of scholarships on a weekly or monthly basis. This means less time searching and more time filling out scholarships.

One thing to note: Scholarships are awarded for many different things, not just GPA. Just because you don't have a top GPA doesn't mean there are not scholarships available for you. They have some crazy scholarships out there like some for left-handed people, or one for making a duct tape dress for prom. Don't avoid searching for scholarships because you think you are not good enough. Donors know the students that are in the top of their class usually receive a large amount of scholarships. That is why they create scholarships that can be earned for things other than GPA.

Scholarship applications should be your main part-time

job. Obviously if you have a real part-time job that comes first, but you should be setting aside several hours a week to fill out scholarship applications. Scholarships can be the highest paying part-time job out there. Think about the math. If you take ten hours over a couple weeks to fill out applications, which would probably be between 20-30 applications, and if you earned $1,000, that would be $100 an hour for your time! Where else can you get paid that type of money?!

I know filling out scholarship applications isn't exactly the most exciting thing to do in your down time, but the amount of money you can earn from filling out forms and typing out a few essays is well worth the payout. Also, don't write off the smaller scholarships. $50 and $100 scholarships can add up quickly. Plus, other students might not take the time to fill out applications for the lower-valued scholarships, so you have less competition!

When you get into college, the available scholarships don't end. I wish I would have paid more attention to this. There are still plenty of scholarships available from the college you are attending. Many donors and alumni donate money to the school to help their favorite departments give money to students who are going to school in those departments.

Just like in high school, find your student services or student success center at your college. I interviewed a college graduate on my YouTube channel and he said that the scholarships he earned in college was what made the biggest difference when it came to his student loan debt. Most of his college scholarships came directly from his school. The scholarships were for students that had great leaderships qualities. In the end, they nearly cut his student debt in half!

If you aren't spending time looking into scholarships, start doing research now. Sign up for multiple sites and start building that relationship with your school counselor. Free money is a great thing—you will thank yourself later when your student loan debt is a lot smaller!

Picking a College

Picking the "right" college can be one of the most stressful parts of the entire process. You want to find a college that you'll enjoy. It has to be in a good location. You want to be with friends. You want it to be affordable. It has to have a good program for your major. You don't want it too big, or too small, you want it just right. Oh, and you want to be able to get accepted into the college. This sounds like a story of Goldilocks and the three colleges!

The point is, there are a lot of factors to look at when picking a college. There are also a lot of influences that may make it difficult to make a decision. By influences, I mean people. Your parents may want you to go to the college they went to. Your friends want you to go to the college they are picking. At the end of the day, the most important person to make this decision is *you*.

You are going to be spending four (or more) years at this place. You want to make sure it's a great (not perfect) fit. One thing that will start making the decision easier is a college visit. Visiting a college can make you fall in love with the campus or it might make you realize this college isn't for you.

When making your list, I usually recommend a list of five or more schools. You will want a couple of *safety* schools. These are schools that you know you are most likely qualified (or overqualified) for based on their acceptance criteria. If you have test scores and a GPA several points above their minimum acceptance criteria, these are going to be your safety schools.

You'll also have some *stretch* schools. These are usually going to be a little bit bigger with slightly higher acceptance criteria. Your test scores and GPA will probably be just above their criteria. These colleges might be some of your favorite colleges where you feel most comfortable. Apply to these early so you can get responses earlier. You don't want to be waiting for an acceptance letter and lose your chance to get into another school if you unfortunately get a rejection letter.

Reach schools are typically your Ivy League schools. They have a very low acceptance rate (under 15%). These schools are very selective in allowing admittance and usually this comes down to their essay. They are looking for top-level students with interesting backgrounds. Grades alone will not guarantee acceptance into these schools. If you want to apply to a reach school do it early, but do not rely heavily on getting accepted to these schools. I've seen many students who say no to their safety school while waiting for an acceptance letter from a reach school, to then be stuck without a school to attend at all.

Top Factors

My three top factors for picking a school are location, cost, and atmosphere. Yours might be different, but it is important to list what your main priorities are going to be. If a school has a great atmosphere but is very expensive and not in the best location, then it might get bumped off the list.

If you want to stay close to family, location might be your number one factor. If cost is your number one factor, you will most likely want to stay within your state lines. Most college costs almost double as soon as you go out of state. When comparing costs, make sure you account for financial aid.

In many cases, more expensive colleges offer higher financial aid, which makes the final cost more comparable with other colleges. This is another reason to make sure your FAFSA is all filled out. After you apply, if you are accepted, you will usually receive a financial aid offer with your acceptance letter.

One factor that I typically put at the bottom of the list is the "brand" of the college. Some people love going to Ivy League colleges because of the name. Saying you graduated from Harvard sounds great, but the cost you have at the end is less than great. You can be a superstar at almost any college you go to as long as you show up and put in the work. I would rather be a big fish in a small pond instead of the other way around.

I went to a local commuter school but because I built up good relationships with my teachers and learned a lot about the local workforce, I was able to secure a job quickly. I also wasn't competing with as many high-level people for the jobs at graduation. Can you imagine competing with other Harvard graduates for a job? Dave Ramsey has a great quote stating, "You never ask a doctor where they went to school before getting a checkup!" If you build the skills and show your value, the name of the school on your resume won't really matter. Make sure you're not making your final decision based off the name of the school.

It is always great to discuss all of these factors and decisions with family, but again, the final decisions would really belong to the student. You can check out ratings and reviews online on sites like collegeboard.com. It is also good to talk to students while on campus visits. Some sources rate colleges higher because they get paid by those colleges. The best source of college life is directly from students that already attend.

Summary

✓ Spend time deciding which college you want to go to.

✓ Pay attention to costs.

✓ Scholarships are free money!

✓ Fill out the FAFSA early!

Finding Your First Job

"If you find a job you love,

You will never work again"

- **Winston Churchill**

One of the number one reasons students go to college after high school is to secure a "good job." The problem is, this job is never guaranteed. This means that even after you spend four or more years in school and tens of thousands of dollars, you could still have a problem securing a job with your degree.

Sometimes the problem is around the major. Other times it may be because of the location you live, which is fortunately easy to change. There are other factors too that may make it more difficult to land a job in the field you want—but know that just when you think all the hard work of school is over, it isn't.

Landing a great job fresh out of school is going to take some hard work. In some cases, you may have to start working before graduation. The great thing is all of that hard work *will* pay off; you just have to make sure you are pointing all of your efforts in the right direction.

Internships

One great way to get your foot in the door and gain experience at the same time is working at an internship over a summer, or multiple summers, during your college career. Most colleges create relationships with local companies looking to hire internships over the summer. There are also plenty of opportunities outside of your local area that are hiring interns as well.

Securing an internship will be similar to securing a full-time job after graduation. The good thing about internships is the company is not usually looking for a student with on-the-job experience, which is really the whole point of an internship.

Companies like to bring in students to help with projects and attract top minds to their companies. They know that students going through college are learning the latest methods and technologies that could be beneficial to their company in the future. They also get to have work done at a cheaper rate than their full-time employees. This is great for you because the company is benefiting as much as you are.

Finding an internship will be similar to finding a job.

Spending time on sites like Indeed, monster.com, and ZipRecruiter are all great sites that will connect you with companies hiring interns. Some companies even go to college fairs to make hiring decisions on the spot.

If you are looking to find a summer internship you should start your search in the fall or early winter. Filling intern positions takes time, and companies want to make sure they have all of their positions filled way before the summer starts.

When picking an internship, pay attention to what you will be working on and what the program is like. If it is local, you only have to worry about traveling back and forth. If the internship is far away, you'll have to look into a place to stay for the summer. I was fortunate enough that during my internship program, the company paid for interns to stay at a nearby college campus for the summer.

Check out what type of work you will be doing. The point of the internship is for you to learn and grow experience in the field you are going to college for, not fetch coffee and hang around in the office all day. If you work hard at the internship, you will already have a great list of bullet points to add to your resume for experience, giving you a major advantage over other applicants that don't have internship experience.

After applying to multiple internships, wait to see if

anyone reaches out for an interview. If a week or two has gone by since you applied and you haven't heard anything, follow up with the internship advisor. If the company has an internship program, the contact information should be easy to find. Show the decision makers that you are very interested and serious about working for that company.

A lot of the information in the rest of this chapter will apply to both internships and job hunting. I really wanted to point out the benefits of an internship and how it can help you land your first job after graduation. Just realize that you should use most of the following information when applying to internships as well as applying to jobs.

Don't Take the First Option That Falls into Your Lap

I am not saying that the first option is a bad option, I just don't want you to instantly say yes when a better option could be right around the corner. If you are applying to multiple companies and multiple companies are contacting you, chances are you could have multiple offers.

Some companies are just looking for almost anyone to come work for their company. This doesn't happen as much with internships as it does with regular entry-level jobs. As soon as you post your resume on a job search site, don't be surprised if you get companies or small businesses calling you for jobs that have nothing to do with your major. Some companies will barely read your resume and just assume you are desperate for a job.

Before you get too far in communication, look up the company on glassdoor.com. This site is a great place to look at reviews from current and past employees. Admittingly, some of the bad reviews are written by upset employees, so they might be written out of emotion rather than fact. I try to look at work/life balance comments as well as culture.

To me, culture at a company is very important. If you aren't going to enjoy the environment you work in every day, you can really start disliking your job quickly. Why spend your time at a place you don't like and probably won't grow in? It is much better to be at a place you enjoy going to where you can see yourself at for ten or more years to come.

As you start your communication with a hiring manager or HR, remember that you are able to dig and get information on the company, just as much as they are trying to dig and get information on you. Finding out how long employees have been working at a place, researching the vacation policy, and really paying close attention to the entire onboarding process can give you a good feel for what it will be like to work at a place.

If a company is disorganized when it comes to setting

up interviews and communicating with you, this might be a red flag of what your work life will be like. I turned down a company because I could sense they were disorganized and that they seemed to be very uptight when it came to rules and processes. I obviously understand all companies have to have rules, but there should also be a sense of empowerment towards the employees to be able to make decisions. The company I was talking with seemed to be very black and white and stuck to a very strict "rulebook." I had a feeling there might have been some friction in the future had I chosen to work there.

Use a Job Recruiter

Using a person who makes a living off of finding other people jobs can be a great way to help get your foot in the door. Sometimes these are called "headhunters," and don't always have the best reputation. Depending on the industry, a headhunter can really make finding a job a lot easier.

I landed both my jobs in software development using a headhunter. With my first job, the company wasn't the best, and they were just trying to talk to as many candidates as possible so they could get them in front of the company. There wasn't much filtering of candidates, so I wasn't fully prepared for my interview. Luckily I got the job, but found out later there were definitely some stronger companies out there.

Headhunters are great because they already have an established relationship with a company. They are just as passionate about you getting hired as you are because they make a commission for the hire. Headhunters should be completely free to the candidate. Sometimes at higher-stakes jobs, candidates may pay for a service, but fresh out of college, this will be a free and very strong resource.

Headhunters will reach out to you usually with a description of a job at a company they represent. They will most likely spend a half hour on the phone with you asking some questions to see if you qualify for the job, and if you do, they'll start moving forward to getting you in for an interview.

Pay close attention to the job description if you are using a headhunter. A lot of the time, these positions may be a "contract-to-hire." This means that there is usually a period of three to six months where you are labeled as a contractor, which can then turn into a full-time position. This allows the hiring company to "test the waters" without having to fully commit.

I was a contract-to-hire at my first job. This is the way the company did almost all of their hires. It sounded scary at first, but I quickly found out that nearly everyone converted to full-time after several months. During that time, I got paid hourly through the headhunter company and had to handle my own health insurance. These are just some of the possible downsides from going through a headhunter company.

On the plus side, I found out about a company I wouldn't have heard about on my own. I also was able to get an interview pretty quickly, compared to applying through an online portal and being added to a "stack" of resumes and applications. The headhunter company was also able to pre-screen me and pass on all of the positive information they found after talking to me, so I was going into the interview with a positive reputation.

Summary

✓ Finding a job is hard work
✓ Put in the time to find a job you enjoy
✓ Looking into using a headhunter

Creating a Great Resume

"When love and skill work together,

Expect a masterpiece"

- **John Ruskin**

The top principles you are going to need in order to land your first job out of school are resume and interview skills. These are the skills that can make the difference between you getting hired for a great job or being stuck in a continuous search for one.

Without a resume or interview, it is nearly impossible to get hired into a company. Even if you would be a great employee at a company, if you aren't great at interviewing, you may be turned down for the job. Fortunately, there is a list of ways you can improve your resume and interview skills that I will lay out in the next two chapters.

The Resume

Your resume is the very first chance that hiring companies have to meet you and look at your list of skills. Most times, your resume is mixed in with a large stack of other resumes. Hiring managers can spend as little as ten seconds looking at your resume, so you must impress them quickly. Your resume will be one page that lists out all your top qualities in an easy-to-read format.

As you get close to graduation, you should start preparing an outline for your resume. Unfortunately, you may not have much job experience, so you will have to dig deeper or get creative for items to add to your resume. You will want to write down a list of extracurricular activities you participated in during high school and college. Any volunteer opportunities or organizations you are involved with should be noted too.

Your goal is to show how busy and how hard of a worker you are. Employers want to see that you can balance multiple responsibilities and not just do the minimum. If you are a couple of years out from graduation, and you realize you are not really involved in anything other than school, you should start looking at activities that you will enjoy that you can add to your resume.

I know some majors may require a little more of your time than others. I also know that everyone has at least fifteen or more hours a day to balance multiple tasks. A friend of mine went to school for pharmacy, which is an extremely difficult major. She worked at a pharmacy as a pharmacy tech part-time. This helped her gain experience and understand how pharmacists worked on a day-to-day basis. On top of learning, her experience was also a great feature to add to her resume.

I talked earlier about internships and how great they are. In my opinion, internships on your resume are a huge attention-grabber! The fact that you worked full-time for an entire summer (or multiple summers) means you learned hands-on experience instead of obtaining information from a book. The other great thing is you can list out multiple lines on your resume covering everything you worked on at the internship, which fills up white space.

Your number one goal with your resume should be to *fill white space*. When that hiring manager is spending just seconds looking at your resume, if they see a lot of white space, they assume you have little experience and haven't done much. If you fill up an entire page with nothing but text listing out all your skills and experience, it's going to grab the attention of the person reading it.

A resume isn't something you can spend just a short amount of time on before submitting it to different companies. You should be spending a large amount of time on this. At least two to four hours. After you have your "rough draft," have others look over it. Most colleges have a career services department or a student success department. In those departments, they should have someone that will help look over your resume and give you tips and guide you on how you can improve what you have done with your resume. They have seen hundreds, if not thousands, of resumes. They also help with what different resumes will look like based on a student's major.

Basic layout

Resumes can have many different looks. If you look online for templates of resumes, you can see all the ways you can format one. If you are looking online for resume templates, make sure you don't copy and paste everything. By doing that, your resume could look just like another resume in the stack. Remember—you want yours to stand out!

Even though there are plenty of different layouts for a resume, you want to make sure your resume has the main sections listed below.

Header

The hiring company needs a way to contact you. Make sure your name, phone number, and email are listed across the top in an easy-to-read font. You want this to be easy to find, but not take up too much room. You need space for the rest of your resume.

Make sure you have a professional email address. The email you used in high school newbsForBreakfast@aol.com or JonasBros4Lyfe@hotmail.com are not going to cut it. The best format is firstname.lastname@gmail.com (maybe with a number or two). Gmail is a free service and is most commonly used. Make sure you check this email daily. You would hate to miss out on an opportunity because you forgot to check your email.

Profile or Summary

This is a sentence or two describing who you are. This, to me, is one of the hardest sections to write. You want it to be a summary of who you are, but not repeat everything that you have listed out in your experience on the resume.

This is typically written in the third person describing what type of employee you are and what kind of experience you are looking to obtain. My profile, when I was looking for computer programming jobs, was:

"Customer-focused information technology professional with additional background in mechanical engineering technology seeking opportunities to maximize capacity for personal growth."

You can see that I laid out who I was and where my focus was. Don't get too wordy with your profile. Remember, hiring managers are not spending a lot of time looking at each individual resume. You want them to understand the value you're going to bring quickly so they'll keep reading and bring you in for an interview.

List your Technical Skills

Some jobs require specific skills that are typically laid out in the job posting. Make sure you are listing these skills on your resume, but only if you have them. Nothing is worse than lying about skills that you do not actually have. Managers will be able to see through that very quickly, especially if you are applying for a technology-related job.

In my technology industry resume, I listed out different software I was familiar with. I mention I am skilled in the entire Microsoft office suite. I also list different programming languages I know. Hopefully you have learned some needed skills in the industry you are applying to. In some cases, you may have to teach yourself some of these skills before applying to different companies.

Education

The next section you can put on your resume is your education. This will include your college and high school graduation. Depending on how much white space will be on your resume, you may not have to list your high school education. If you graduated college, it is assumed that you also graduated high school. List your major, the college you graduated from, and the GPA you received at graduation. If your GPA isn't higher than a 3.0, I wouldn't list it on your resume. Not that below a 3.0 is a bad thing, but we want to highlight all of your top achievements.

Make sure to **bold** your college. Again, remember—this one-page resume is going to have a lot of different text on it. You want to make it easily readable for any manager looking over it.

Work Experience

This is one of the more important sections on your resume. This is where companies get to see what you have been working on in the past. This shows them how hard of a worker you are and how much value you will be able to add to their organization.

If you completed an internship, this will be where your resume can shine. List all your high school and college jobs. This will show that you were able to balance a job while going to school full-time. List them in order from most recent to furthest in the past.

Under each job, add bullet points explaining what you accomplished while there. If you have a current job, all lines will read *present* tense. All past jobs will read *past* tense. Make sure to list the dates you worked at each job. If, for some reason, you were at a job for a short time and it didn't work out, you don't have to list that experience. Also, the internship will obviously only be a few months long, so that can stay.

Try to be creative when listing your tasks and experience at each job. Don't start off each sentence with the same word. You may want to use a thesaurus for some descriptive words. For instance, if you had a customer service job, instead of just saying "helped," you can use other words like "supported." If you had any leadership responsibilities make sure they are located at the top of the list. Your tasks and experience for each job will help you fill in more white space. Just make sure you are not repeating a responsibility, but wording it differently.

Activities and Volunteer Experience

If you are still looking to fill white space you can list out any activities or volunteer experiences you had in college and/or high school. These can be organizations you participated in. Again, if you held a leadership role for any of these organizations, make sure to list that at the top. National Honor Society, student government, and nonprofit organizations are all great organizations to be a part of and to list on your resume.

This should give you a basic outline of how to lay out your resume. Remember, you want this resume to stand out. Make sure the sections are easy to identify. You can add horizontal lines to establish the header of each section. Use different fonts to represent different importance levels. Anything important you want seen should be bolded. On my resume I bolded the name of each company I worked for.

You can still get a great idea of how resumes should look online if you just search for resume templates. You should never pay for a resume template though. Just realize you do not want your resume to look boring and like every other resume out there. Get help where you can.

The summary profile is a great place to get help from others. Have others read your experience to make sure lines don't come across as repetitive. A resume is the very first and important step in getting a job. Without a good resume, your chances of landing an interview will be difficult.

Want a template of my personal resume for a starting spot? Download the template and other bonuses at StudentSucessPrinciples.com

Summary

- ✓ Your resume is your first impression at a hiring company
- ✓ Fill up as much white space as possible
- ✓ List as many valuable skills as possible
- ✓ Have others look at your resume

Interviewing

"Job Interviews are like first dates

Good impressions count.

Awkwardness may occur.

Outcomes are unpredictable."

-   **anonymous**

Now that you have an awesome resume, the next step in getting your first big job out of school will be an interview. Interviews are honestly my favorite part of the application process. I can only sell myself so much on a piece of paper. In an interview you get the chance to show the company how great of an employee you can be. They get to see more of your personality and passion for the job you are applying for.

Professional Voicemail

The first thing to know about getting an interview is the screening process actually starts *before* you walk through the doors of the company. Some companies want to see how well you handle communication and organization. Before you submit applications, you should make sure you have a professional voicemail message. If you miss the phone call, this will be the first impression the company gets to interact with, other than your resume.

It isn't that hard to record a professional voicemail. You are mostly making sure that your tone comes across confident and easy to understand. Don't record your voicemail going down the highway using Bluetooth. Thank the caller for giving you a call and apologize for not being able to answer it. Ask them to leave a name and a number and you'll return their call as quickly as possible.

During your job-hunting period, make sure you are checking your voicemails every day. Your smartphone should notify you of a new voicemail, but I wouldn't trust it. You do *not* want to keep companies waiting for you to return their call.

On another note, I would try to answer any call that comes in. Make sure you are in a quiet area when answering.

Assume that every call you don't recognize is a hiring manager on the other end. Sure, you may answer some calls from salespeople, but you want to get in contact with a hiring company as quickly as possible.

Organized Schedule

When that calls comes in, you need to have a full understanding of what your schedule is at all times. Make sure you know your current work schedule, as well as any other obligations in your phone calendar. The person calling you will want to set up a time for a first interview. You want to show them you manage your time well and know everything that is happening in your life. One of the worst things you can do would be to forget about an important responsibility and have to call the company to reschedule. Remember, they are watching, and listening, to everything you do from the first contact.

Preparing

Depending on the company and the job, you could be interviewing with one person one time, or you could be interviewing with multiple people multiple times. It is very common now to interview with more than one person.

The company or team you are interviewing for wants multiple people to check in and make sure you are a good fit for their culture, team, and have the skills to succeed.

If you haven't been to an interview in a long time, you will want to start getting a list of potential questions the company may ask. You can search in google to find these in many cases. For instance, being in computer programming, if you search for "interview questions for a software developer" you'll get plenty of examples of what could be asked.

If you are interviewing with a larger company, check out their site on glassdoor.com. This site lists salaries, the happiness of the employees, as well as *experiences from previous interviews*. Some users may even list the questions they were asked during the interview, or at the very least, comment on how many people they interviewed with and the process.

The more prepared you are, the easier the interview will be. It is also not a bad idea to look up information about the company. Look up how long they've been in business, how much they've grown over the years. Make sure you really understand the product they deliver and how the position you are applying for helps them deliver that product.

Some of this may seem pretty simple. Looking up facts on a company doesn't take much time, but you would be surprised how many candidates do not even take the time to do something so small. Even if you study directly from the company's website, you are showing initiative and passion for the company you are about to potentially work for.

If your position has a lot of technical skills required, try to brush up on those skills you have learned in school. The job posting should list out expected qualifications and knowledge base. Focus on those areas as you prepare for the interview. You may not be an expert in every area, and that is okay. You can acknowledge the fact you don't have the full knowledge of some areas but are looking to learn and grow. You obviously can't do this for *everything* they need. If you don't have at least average knowledge on most of the topics, you shouldn't be applying for that position.

The Day Of

When the big day finally comes, chances are you will be pretty nervous. Being the center of attention while talking to a hiring manager can be pretty nerve-racking, but you cannot let that slip you up. The night before, make sure you get plenty of sleep. You do not want to show up looking like a zombie! The more awake you are, the more confident you will look to the hiring manager.

Make sure your outfit is also picked out *and prepared* the night before. This means clothes ironed out and hung up. Make sure your dress shoes still fit and don't have any scuffs on them. You do not want the nightmare of trying to find a working iron in the morning or realize that your dog was chewing on your only pair of dress shoes an hour before you have to leave.

Different jobs have different dress codes. If you can, research what type of dress code the company has. You may be able to find out if they post pictures of employees on their website. Some companies brag about their laid-back culture. This doesn't mean you get to show up in a t-shirt and flip flops. However, showing up in a professional three-piece suit may be a little over the top. If you are communicating with the human resources department before the interview, you may even ask what their typical employee dress code is.

Guys will most likely wear a button-down shirt with a tie. You may also wear a vest, if that is something you normally wear on a nice night out. For ladies, a nice dress or longer skirt with a blouse will work. You can google plenty of dress code ideas for all of the different industries and you will get a laundry list of ideas. Don't spend too much focus on this, just make sure you show up looking professional.

If you are traveling more than thirty minutes away, make sure you give yourself *plenty* of time to get there. My first job was sixty miles away. I left almost two hours before the interview started. I wasn't familiar with the area, so wanted to make sure I could find it. I also didn't know what the construction situation would be like. It is always better to be safe than sorry. Showing up late to an interview gives a very bad first impression.

No matter how far away the interview is, you should be parked in their parking lot at least fifteen minutes before the interview. That'll give you time to mentally prepare for the interview and walk in ten minutes before it starts. Trust me when I tell you that many people today do not understand the importance of time! Arriving ten minutes early demonstrates that you know how to be prepared and you respect the time of the people interviewing you.

Make sure you take everything you will need. If possible, lay it out the night before. If a company has an odd procedure, they will give you instructions on extra things to bring.

Some basic things you should bring with you are:

> Photo ID — Some companies need this to check you in.
> Cash — For a parking garage as well as a debit card.
> Umbrella — You don't want to show up soaking wet if there is a long walk from the parking lot to the building.
> Resume — Most companies will bring this, but again there is no harm in being over-prepared.

Make sure your cell phone is fully charged, or you have a phone charger in your car. Your phone will stay in the car during your interview, but just in case something happens before you get there, you'll need your phone to call the company to let them know. Make sure you have a phone number of a contact person on the off chance that this happens.

When you arrive at the area in the building you need to be, walk up to the receptionist, make great eye contact, and let them know who you are and who you are there to see. You never know who reports back during your interview process. You will most likely be seated until that person arrives. During this time, you can continue mentally preparing for the interview. Your phone should be in the car; don't have any gum in your mouth and make sure, if you are nervous, your hands aren't getting sweaty. You are about to shake hands with the interviewer and don't want to shake their hands with your clammy hands.

Handshakes

There isn't a whole lot to be said about handshakes. I know it sounds weird to have a sub section about it, but again, the handshake, if done wrong, could put you off to a bad start. As mentioned above, make sure your hand is clean from sweat or dirt. When you approach the hiring manager, make sure to hold eye contact and give them a solid and confident handshake. The one analogy I love to use is make sure you don't give them a "dead fish" handshake. That is where you just hold your hand up, and let them basically shake your hand, as if there is nothing attached to it. I am not saying you have to squeeze their hand until it turns red, just make sure they feel some energy.

During the Interview

You have finally made it back to the office where they'll be conducting the interview. You may be sitting across from one person, one-on-one, or you may be in a panel interview where there are multiple people sitting across from you. Both follow the same process, so the only thing that changes for you is where you direct your attention.

Obviously, in a one-on-one you can talk directly to the one person across from you. Hold eye contact as much as possible and talk just like you would with a group of friends. Obviously, eliminate any slang terms you would use with your friends. In a panel interview, you should always start with your attention given to the person who is asking a question, but make sure as you express your answer, you are talking to the others across the table, making eye contact one person at a time.

When sitting in your chair, be sure you have good

posture. Both feet on the ground and back up straight or leaning forward. You should *never* be leaning back in your chair. If you look too comfortable and laid back, they will think you are not interested. It is great if you are relaxed, but you need to be showing full attention and listening to everything they say.

Interviews are basically a series of them asking questions and you answering. The questions they ask shouldn't be simple yes/no answers. They want you to elaborate on your answer. Give details and use examples. The more details you give, the easier it'll be for them to understand the situation, and the more credibility it adds to your answer. It is okay to take a few seconds before giving an answer. If you just spurt out the first thing that comes to mind, the answer may fall short.

If you can't immediately think of an answer, you can respond with a "That is a great question, and I have a few answers to that, let me think of the best way to put this." The interviewers understand that you are most likely nervous. Talking a little bit while thinking of an answer works, sitting there and only saying "Umm," does not work.

If you don't know the answer to a question, say that you don't know the answer. You can say something like "I'm sorry, I don't really know the answer to that question, but I know that I could find it if I had a few minutes to learn." It is obviously great if you know the answer to every question, but it can't be expected. A lot of times, companies want to see how you answer the question, or how you arrive at an answer. There are many great interview questions out there that don't actually have an answer. The interviewer wants to see how you work to come up with one.

One of my favorite questions is "How many inflated balloons can you fit in a school bus?" Who knows what the real answer is. This always leads to questions like "Are there seats inside?" or "Is it a normal-sized school bus?" Just giving an answer of 20,000 doesn't work either. You want to talk through all of your calculations. Talk about multiplying the length, width, and height of the bus.

Estimate that a balloon holds about one cubic foot of air and figure out roughly how many cubic feet are in that bus. I have heard some crazy answers that can't be anywhere close to accurate, BUT they talked through the problem step-by-step, and those steps made sense.

Bring Questions

This company is interviewing you, just as much as you are interviewing them. As you walk through the office, look at the layout. Is this somewhere you could see yourself working for the next several years? How are people dressed? Do they seem happy? These are things that should be going through your head as you walk through the office on your way to the interview.

As your interview wraps up, they may ask if you have any questions for them. Try to make a list of questions you would like answers to. Ask them what their favorite part of working there is. Ask them what a typical day looks like for employees. Make questions you are genuinely curious about. I really try to make sure I don't answer with "Nope, no questions from me."

Questions show curiosity and interest in their company, plus you are getting answers that help you decide if you want to work somewhere. I mentioned in a previous chapter questions like this helped me decide between two job offers I had. If I didn't ask these questions, it would have been a flip of a coin, which could have landed wrong.

Don't ask about compensation yet, that will come later with a job offer. You can ask about how long before you hear back from them. Don't be too pushy with this, just show you are eager to work for them and want to start adding value soon.

Video Interviews

As technology continues to grow, and jobs are now

hiring from all parts of the country or even the world, the chance of conducting a video interview is increasing. I enjoy these because they don't require you to travel or have to worry about traffic or finding a parking spot. Everything I laid out above still holds true. You will want to make more eye contact with your camera though, rather than the person on screen.

The one area that is different with a video interview is the technology needed to conduct the interview. Today most companies will be using Skype, Zoom, or a WebEx. They should send you instructions on everything you need in order to connect with them on the interview day. MAKE SURE YOU TEST THIS BEFORE THE INTERVIEW. If you need to, have a friend download the software and call them. You want to know how to handle the audio and video on your computer.

For audio, try to use the earbuds that have a microphone on them. I am not talking about large gaming headphones. I am talking about the earbuds you would plug into a smartphone. Make sure you have a good quiet spot in your house with great lighting. You obviously aren't making a professional video for YouTube, but a bad connection can be a real distraction for the interviewer. Test all of this technology with a friend. Make sure they can easily hear and see you on their end.

Just like a normal interview, show up fifteen minutes before and connect to the interview. The interviewer may not be there yet, but you'll know that you are fully connected and where you need to be. When the interviewer comes on, say hello with a smile and that it is great to meet them. Pay attention to how you look on camera. Make sure you are fully in frame and that no pets will be popping up during your interview.

After the Interview

This may be the hardest part of the interview. Sure, you can now breathe easily since it is all over, but the waiting game can feel like forever. In some cases, you may have a strong feeling on how the interview went. If you couldn't answer any questions, it probably didn't go so well. Don't let the way you feel dictate your expectations. I've heard of many students thinking they bombed an interview, to get a job offer the next day. I have also had students that were very confident, but didn't receive an offer.

One more piece that can make you stand out from the crowd: Find out the contact information of the person(s) that interviewed you and send them a thank you note. This is something not a lot of people do, and this made a big difference when I was applying for my internship. Handwritten is the best way to go but, if for some reason time is tight, send a nice thank you email to the hiring manager. When I was in my internship at Timken, the coordinator said he kept all of the thank you notes they received from candidates, and out of the thousand that applied, I was one of five that sent a thank you note. Is it kind of brown-nosing? Sure. But it also shows initiative and that you truly care about working at that company. It only takes a few minutes and could make a difference on the final outcome.

You've Got This!

I laid out a lot of different things to think about when landing an interview. I know you won't remember every last detail and that is okay. The point is, the more you focus and prepare for an interview the better off you will do. I can by no means guarantee that you will get every job you interview for. In some cases you are a great candidate, but in others there is another person out there who is a slightly better fit for the company.

This chapter was really to show you some small improvement you can make that will give you an advantage against other candidates. Interviews are your time to shine, and if you make some of these small improvements, you will shine super bright!

Summary

✓ You are being interviewed from the first contact

✓ Plan your interview day the day before

✓ Show up early

✓ Prove to the interviewers how valuable you are

Using the Student Success Principles

"Success is attracted to the person you become"

- Jim Rohn

-

First let me say great job on making it this far! Did you know not everyone actually reads an entire book from beginning to end? In our busy lives it is easy to get distracted and leave a book half-read. I wrote this book and filled it with information in hopes that you would get something out of every chapter. If you are reading this, I am assuming I have achieved that goal.

We have covered a lot in the previous chapters. We started with personal development, moved through finances, and ended up at adulting. Ask most adults what they wished they would have learned more of in school and I can bet that a lot of it is covered in this book.

I have never understood the point of spending years in school learning from books and tests to never get life lessons on how to succeed after graduation. Obviously, school teaches a lot of great skills that you can use in your life and for a future career, but landing that job is never really spelled out.

These principles are a collection of things I have failed at or learned along the way. Some of these principles might not be relevant to you right now and that's fine. Most likely, at some point in your life, ever chapter in this book will be used as you work towards your life after graduation.

Now, just because these principles were written from my experiences does not mean that they won't be a little different for you. I have met many people and read enough books to realize not everyone does time management or goal-setting the same way I do. The biggest takeaway from this book is to put focus into these areas of your life. If you just move through life without a plan, life is going to knock you down.

Even if you have a plan, there are still going to be a lot of ups and downs. Being prepared will help with the rough patches. If you pay attention to many of the successful role models in your life, you will see they are always learning from new experiences. After reading this book, you should start to see there is an endless amount of growth available for you. Just getting by might be comfortable, but not reaching your full potential seems very disappointing to me.

I do not believe humans exist just to fill space. We have

a limitless amount of potential, but if we do not invest in that potential, we won't grow. If we don't grow, our lives will not change much from where they are today. Think about how much you have grown in the last fifteen or more years. That is only a small fraction of your lifetime. Why not start your life after graduation with a great launch? Imagine what you could be if you keep pushing for more.

These principles will not get you to your maximum potential. There are many more life lessons for you to learn. I don't want you spending the first several years after graduation trying to "figure it out." You have put too much time, energy, and money into your life to be here. If you ask a carpenter what makes their job easiest, I am sure they'll answer the tools they use to get the job done.

Use this book as a list of tools to get you started on your journey to a successful life. Use the principles laid out in this book to get you into a job you enjoy, so you can spend more of your energy on yourself rather than draining energy into a job you hate. According to a Gallup Poll[6], over 80% of people worldwide hate their jobs. We spend a lot of our life working. Why should we spend it in a place that drains our energy?

I believe that if you are reading this book, you have the potential for greatness. It is not going to be an easy thing, but by focusing on yourself, you will exponentially grow into successful person day by day. That success will look different for each person; it may be even bigger than you can imagine right now. Dreams will change, but if you focus on your future, it can only grow.

Maybe you do not fully believe in yourself right now. Maybe you don't think it is possible. Why do you think you don't deserve to be as happy as anyone else? There are so many "normal" people out there who grew up in circumstances similar to yours who have created a life of their dreams. They had the motivation and the drive to achieve it, and I know you can too!

As you close this book, dream about where you would like your life to be in the next five to ten years. Dream as big as you can. Your life is just beginning as you walk across that stage. You have barely begun to experience what your life holds. Every achieved goal starts with one step at a time. Use the principles in this book to start paving that path and see where it takes you!

In case you missed them, I have created 5 bonuses for you around this book. To get free access to them go to StudentSucessPrinciples.com!

References

1. 80 percent fail at achieving goals - https://health.usnews.com/health-news/blogs/eat-run/articles/2015-12-29/why-80-percent-of-new-years-resolutions-fail
2. 3% of people write down their goals https://www.forbes.com/sites/annabelacton/2017/11/03/how-to-set-goals-and-why-you-should-do-it/
3. We watch 6 hours a day watching video - https://techcrunch.com/2018/07/31/u-s-adults-now-spend-nearly-6-hours-per-day-watching-video
4. 39% of americans have enough savings to cover $1000 emergency : https://www.cnbc.com/2018/01/18/few-americans-have-enough-savings-to-cover-a-1000-emergency.html
5. $2.6 BILLION went unclaimed by graduates - https://www.nerdwallet.com/blog/loans/student-loans/2018-fafsa-pell-grant/
6. 85% of people hate their jobs - https://returntonow.net/2017/09/22/85-people-hate-jobs-gallup-poll-says/

Success After Graduation

Visit SuccessAfterGraduation.com for more content

Follow me on Instagram and Facebook

@JonClarkSpeaks

Front Row Foundation

Front Row Foundation is a charity I love. This organization helps people who are battling life threatening illnesses and puts them in to the front row at the event of their dreams. Their mission is to shine some light when families are

dealing with dark times.

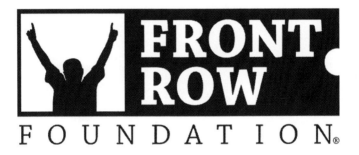

If you would like to find out more information, I highly suggest visiting FrontRowFoundation.org

Made in the USA
Lexington, KY
15 November 2019